100 GREAT COUNTRY SONGS

Editor: Carol Cuellar
Book Design: Joseph Klucar

CONTENTS

SUMMER'S COMIN'

Words and Music by
CLINT BLACK and HAYDEN NICHOLAS

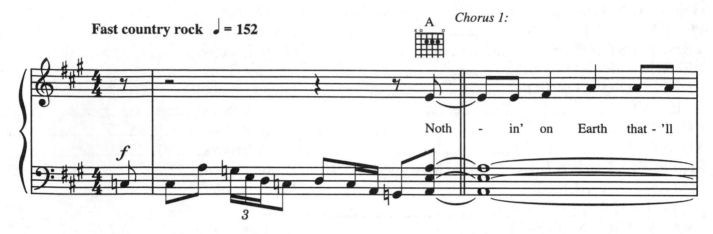

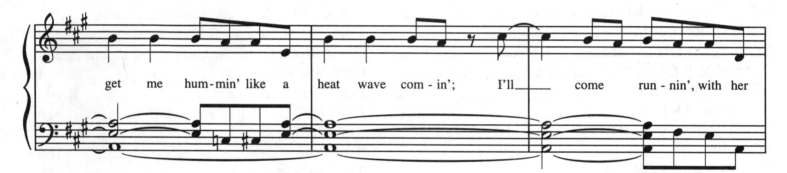

Summer's Comin' - 5 - 1

first one stand-in' in___ line_____ for my day in the sun,___ I've been

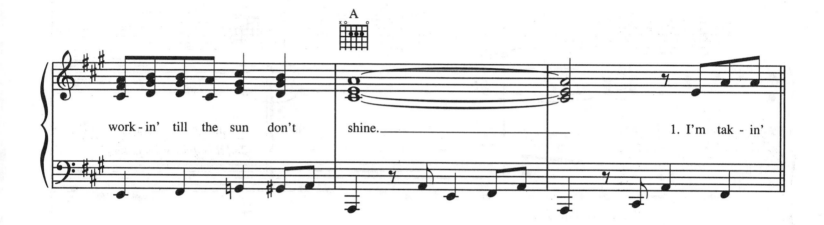

work-in' till the sun don't shine._____ 1. I'm tak-in'

Verse:

off my hat and leave it to the boys, get that old work__ mon-key down__
2. *See additional lyric*

off my___ back. All I want's a lit-tle peace__ and noise,__ hit the

6

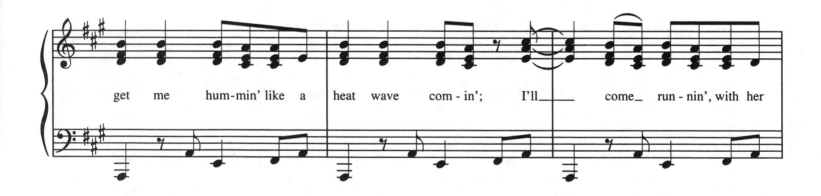

-ur-day night. And ev - ery-thing's_ right with the sum - mer com - in'; I'm the

first one stand-in' in___ line_____ for my day in the sun,___ I've been

1.

N.C.

work-in' till the sun don't shine.

2.   D.S. %   3.

2. When the

...*end solo*)

For my day in the sun,___ I've been

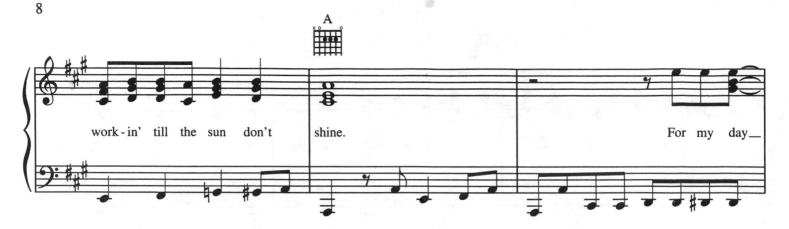

work-in' till the sun don't shine. For my day—

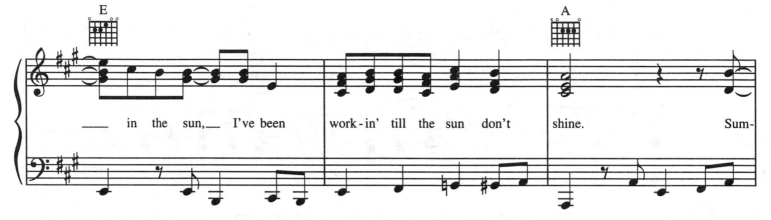

— in the sun,— I've been work-in' till the sun don't shine. Sum-

- mer's com-in', to shine.— Sum - mer's com-in', to shine.— Sum-

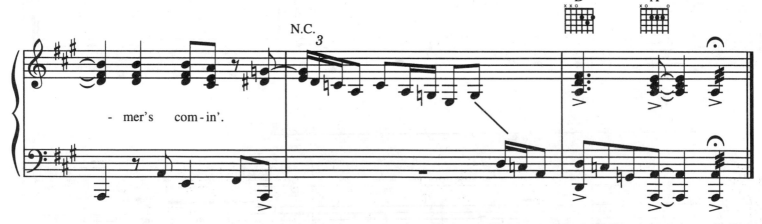

- mer's com-in'.

Verse 2:
When the day gets cookin', gonna grab my toys,
And it really doesn't matter which wave we're on.
Get to turnin' up them good old boys,
Crankin' into the night; by the break of dawn,
All the towns are red and I still see blond.
(To Chorus:)

TILL YOU LOVE ME

Words and Music by
BOB DIPIERO and GARY BURR

Till You Love Me - 3 - 1

Chorus:

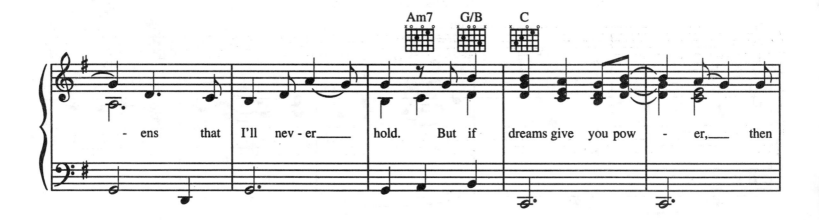

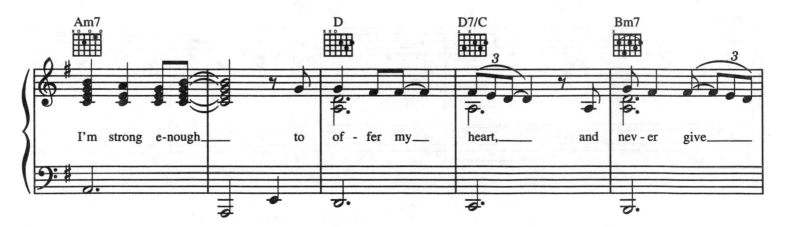

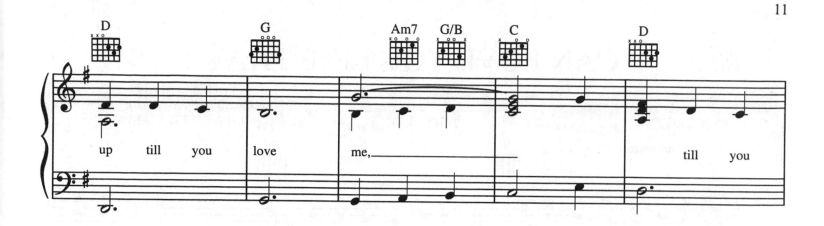

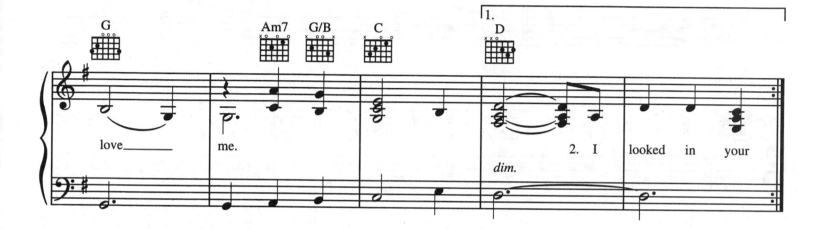

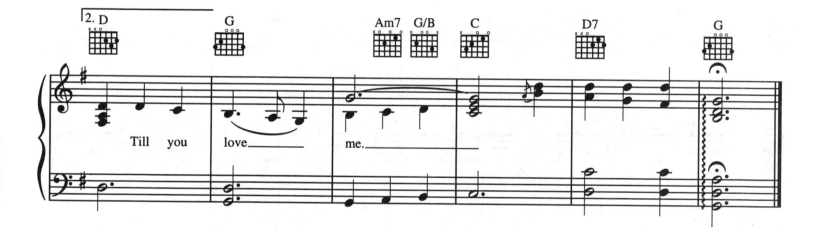

Verse 2:
I looked in your eyes, so bright and so blue.
And that's when I knew that you could be mine.
If good things come to those who wait,
Well, I guess I can wait if that's what I have to do.
Oh, it's worth it for you.
(To Chorus:)

I CAN LOVE YOU LIKE THAT

Words and Music by
STEVE DIAMOND, MARIBETH DERRY
and JENNIFER KIMBALL

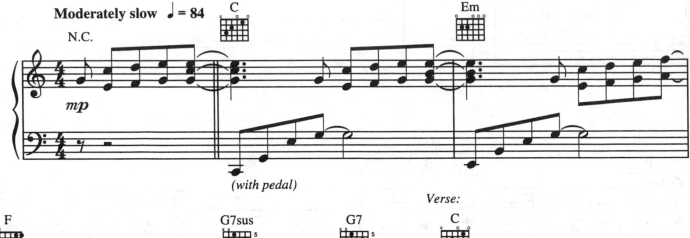

1. They read you Cin-der-el-la, you hoped it would come true,___ that one day your Prince Charm-ing would come_ res-cue you.___ You like ro-man-tic mov-ies, you nev-er will_ for-get the way you felt when Ro-me-o_ kissed_

nev-er make a prom-ise I don't in-tend to keep,___ so when I say for-ev-er, for-ev-er's what I___ mean. I'm no Ca-sa-no-va, but I swear this much_ is true: I'll be hold-ing noth-ing back_ when_

Ju - li - et.___ ___ All this time that you've been wait - ing,___
it comes to___ you. You dream of love that's ev - er - last - ing,___ well

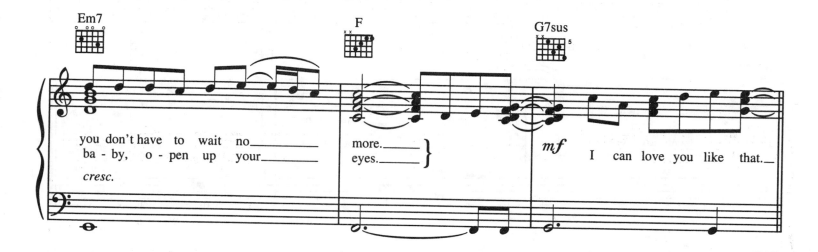

you don't have to wait no___ more.___ *mf* I can love you like that.___
ba - by, o - pen up your___ eyes.___
cresc.

Chorus:

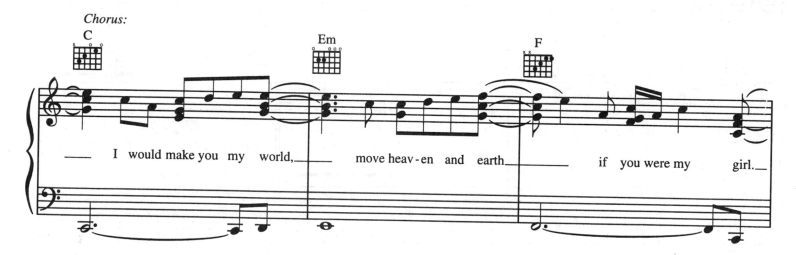

___ I would make you my world,___ move heav - en and earth___ if you were my girl.___

___ I will give you my heart,___ be all that you need,___ show you you're ev -

I Can Love You Like That - 4 - 2

14

- 'ry - thing that's pre-cious to me.___ If you give me a chance,___

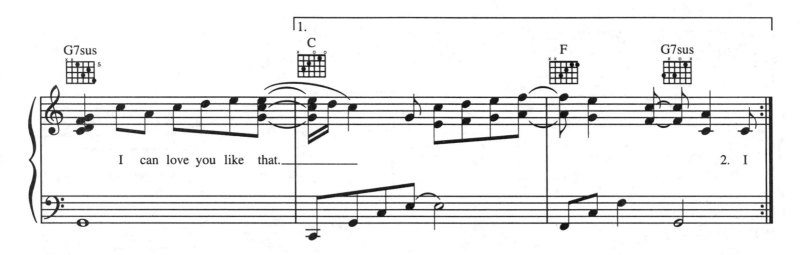

I can love you like that.___ 2. I

___ You want ten-der-ness,___ I've got ten-

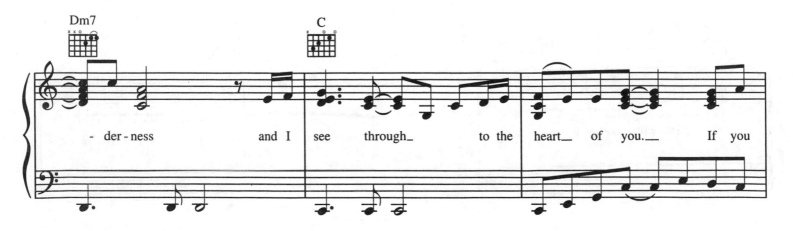

-der-ness and I see through___ to the heart___ of you.___ If you

ANGELS AMONG US

Words and Music by
BECKY HOBBS and DON GOODMAN

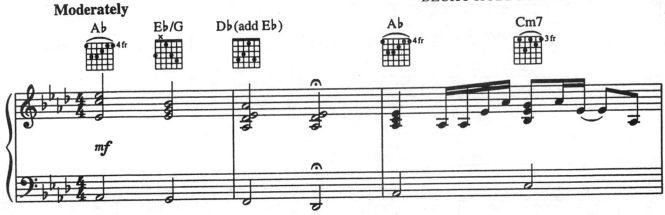

Spoken: *I was walking home from school*
(See additional lyrics)

on a cold winter day,

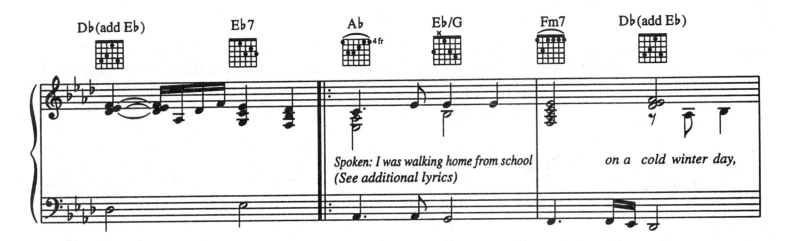

took a short cut through the *woods and I lost my way.* *It was getting late*

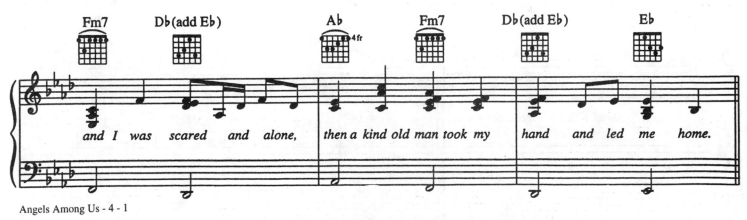

and I was scared and alone, *then a kind old man took my* *hand and led me home.*

Angels Among Us - 4 - 1

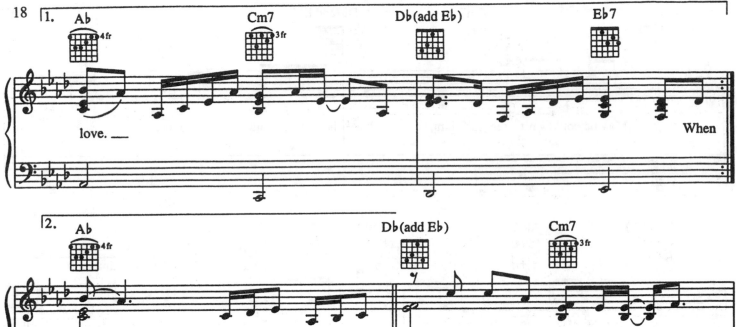

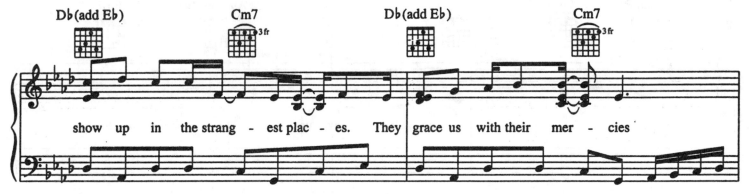

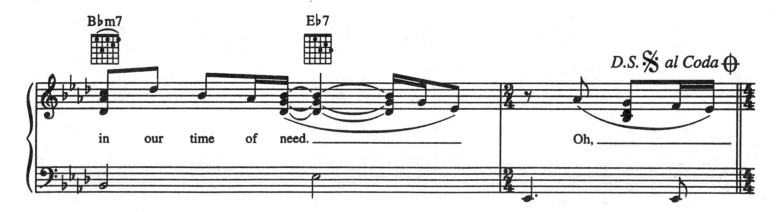

Repeat and fade

I be-lieve there are an-gels a-mong __ us

a tempo

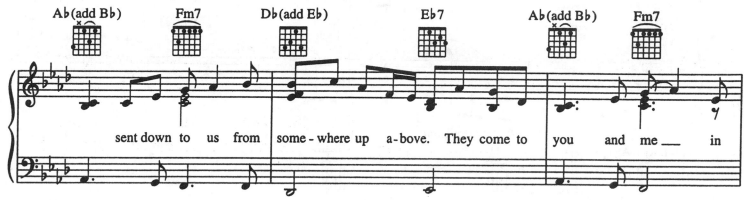

sent down to us from some-where up a-bove. They come to you and me __ in

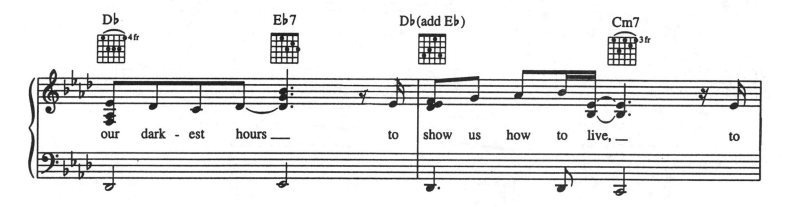

our dark-est hours __ to show us how to live, __ to

teach us how to give _____ to guide us with a light of _____ love. __

Additional lyrics

When life held troubled times and had me down on my knees,
There's always been someone to come along and comfort me.
A kind word from a stranger, to lend a helping hand,
A phone call from a friend just to say I understand.
Now, ain't it kind of funny, at the dark end of the road,
Someone lights the way with just a single ray of hope.

(To Chorus)

I SWEAR

Words and Music by
GARY BAKER and FRANK MYERS

I see the ques - tions in your eyes,
(See additional lyrics)

I know what's weigh - ing on your mind, but you can be sure

I Swear - 4 - 1

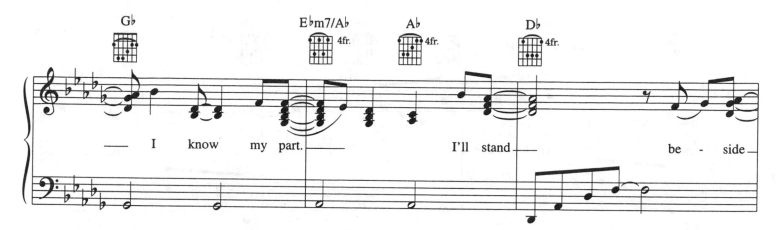

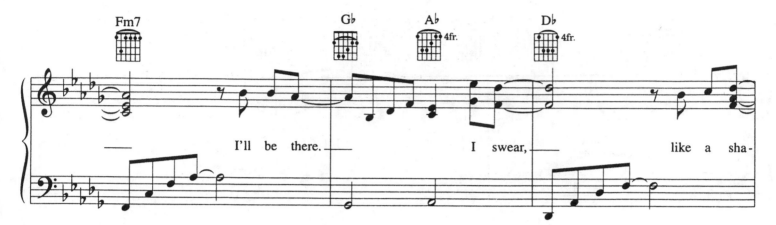

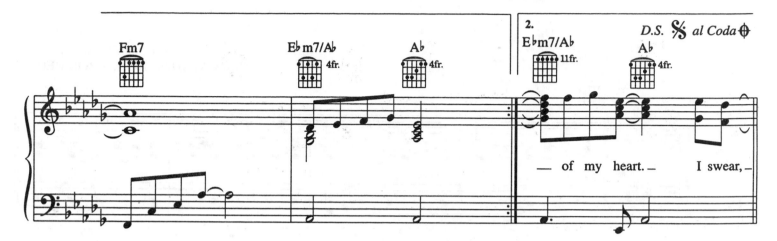

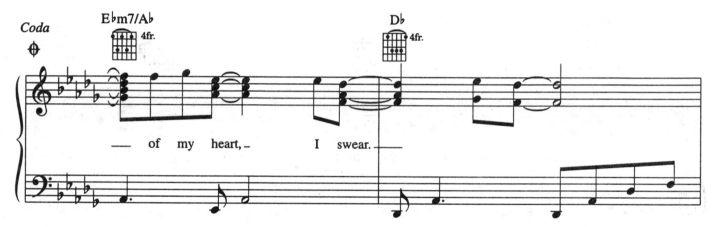

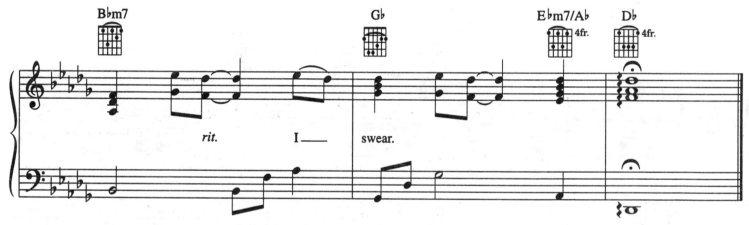

Additional lyrics

2. I'll give you everything I can,
   I'll build your dreams with these two hands,
   And we'll hang some memories on the wall.
   And when there's silver in your hair,
   You won't have to ask if I still care,
   'Cause as time turns the page my love won't age at all.
   (To Chorus)

THINKIN' ABOUT YOU

Words and Music by
TOM SHAPIRO and BOB REGAN

Verse 1:

1. I'm not quite sure what's go-in'___ on,___ but all day through and

all night__ long,__ I've been think-in' a-bout___ you, I've been

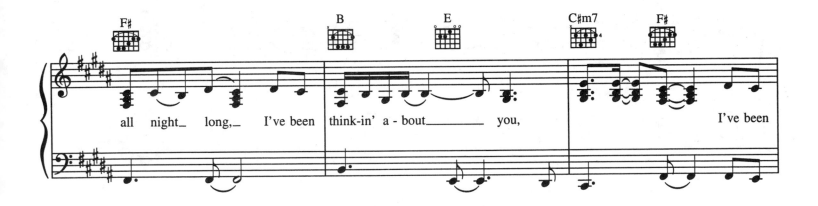

Verse 2:

think-in' a-bout___ you. 2. The look in your eyes when you

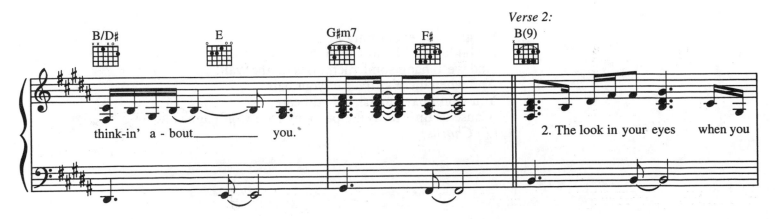

Thinkin' about You - 4 - 1

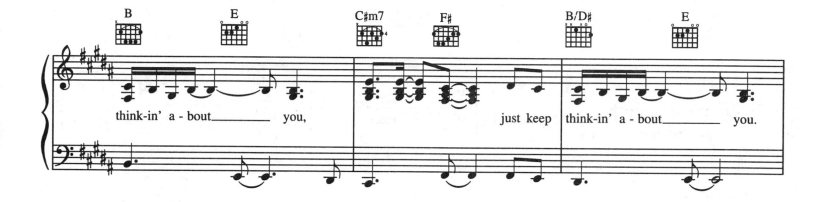

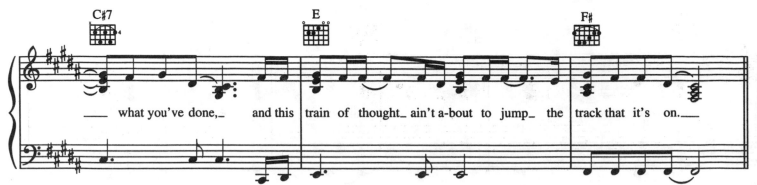

what you've done,____ and this train of thought___ ain't a-bout to jump___ the track that it's on.___

Verses 3 & 4:

3. In the back of my mind, there's a se - cret place.___ But the whole world knows by the

4. *See additional lyrics*

smile on my face____ that I've been think-in' a - bout_____ you.

To Coda ⊕

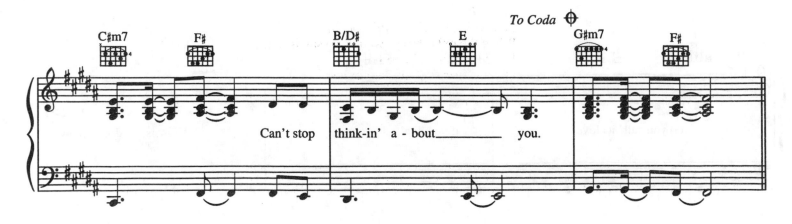

Can't stop think-in' a - bout_____ you.

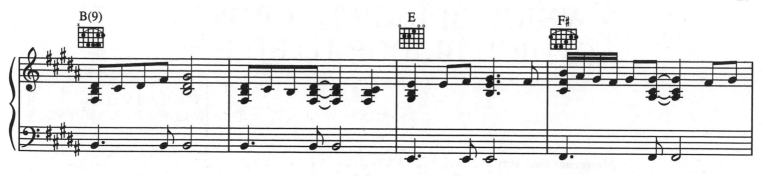

Verse 4:
I know it's crazy, callin' you this late,
When the only thing I wanted to say is that
I've been thinkin' about you,
Oh, just keep thinkin' about you.

WHICH BRIDGE TO CROSS
(WHICH BRIDGE TO BURN)

Words and Music by
VINCE GILL and BILL ANDERSON

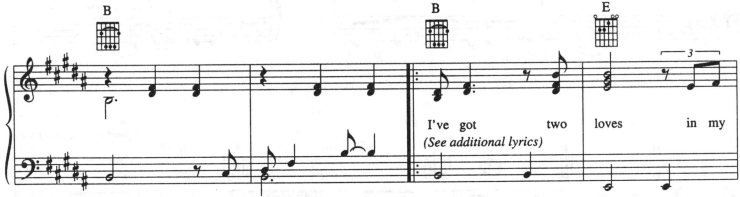

I've got two loves in my
(See additional lyrics)

life now: A true love and one that's brand

new. I'm not real-ly sure— that I

Which Bridge to Cross (Which Bridge to Burn) - 5 - 1

know how to love one and tell one we're

through. I can't sleep at night,—— I

toss and I turn.—— I keep los - ing sight of the

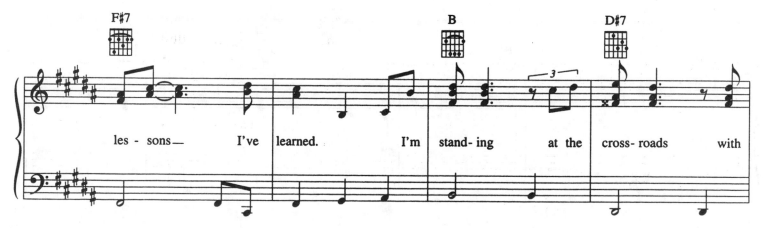

les - sons—— I've learned. I'm stand- ing at the cross- roads with

Which Bridge to Cross (Which Bridge to Burn) - 5 - 2

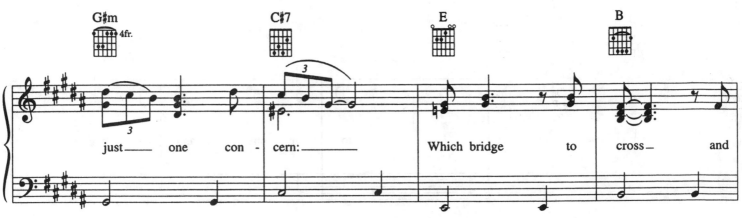

just —— one con - cern: —— Which bridge to cross —— and

which bridge to burn. ————   I

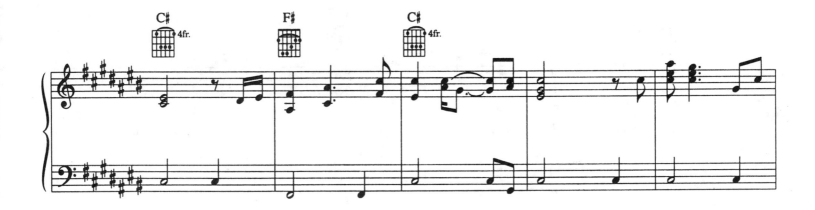

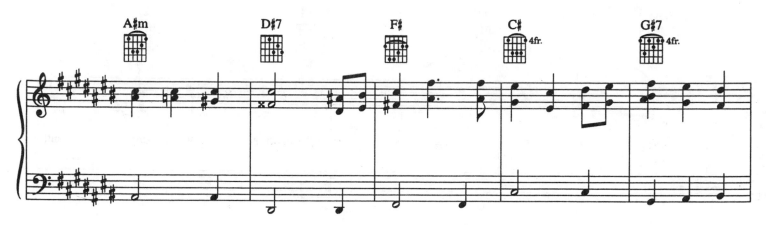

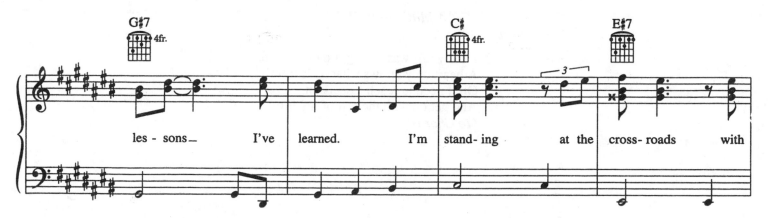

Which Bridge to Cross (Which Bridge to Burn) - 5 - 4

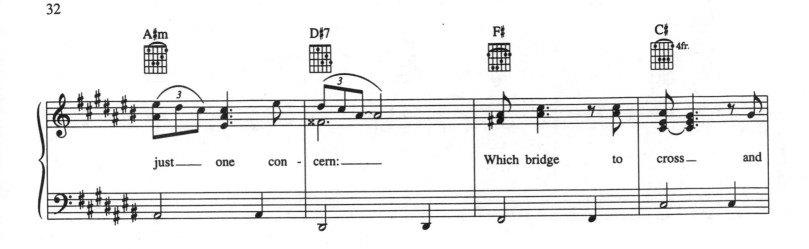

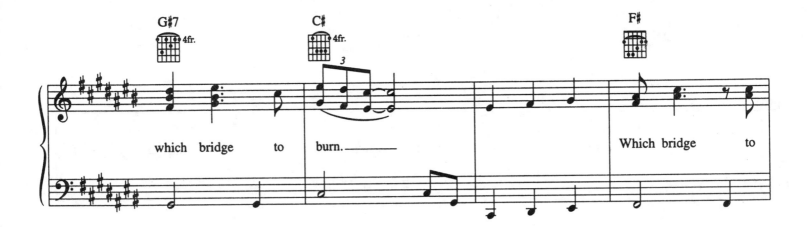

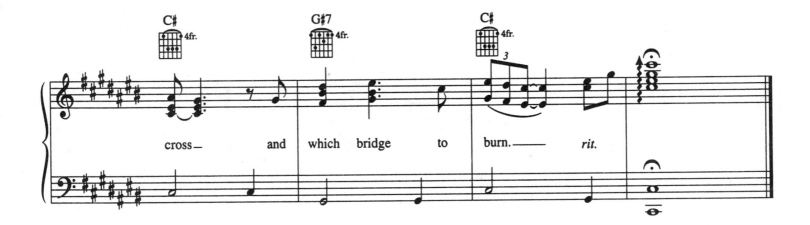

Additional lyrics

2. I knew this was wrong, I didn't listen,
   A heart only knows what feels right.
   Oh, I need to reach a decision,
   And get on with the rest of my life.
   (To Chorus)

AMY'S BACK IN AUSTIN

Written by
BRADY SEALS and
STEPHEN ALLEN DAVIS

Moderately ♩ = 116

1. We left Tex-as on a wind-y night___ in a

beat up Chev-y___ van.___ We load-ed it up with our in-

-no-cent dreams_ and all the love_ we had._ We

Amy's Back in Austin - 5 - 1

did - n't know   then__ how hard__   it was,__   liv - in' on our__ own.__

2. *See additional lyrics*

__   I'd find her cry - ing late__   at night__

talk - in' to the folks back   home.__   I   won - der what__ went wrong__

__   and where__   is she now.__ I'd love__   to__ know.__

%. *Chorus:*

I bet Am-y's back in Aus-tin work-in' at La

f (Instrumental solo 3rd time...

Zo-na Ro-sa Ca-fe. I re-mem-ber the night we lost

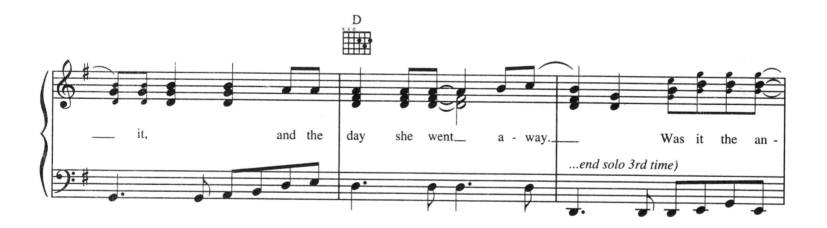

it, and the day she went a-way. Was it the an-

...end solo 3rd time)

-gry words or did she miss her mom-ma? I don't know, but it don't feel right.

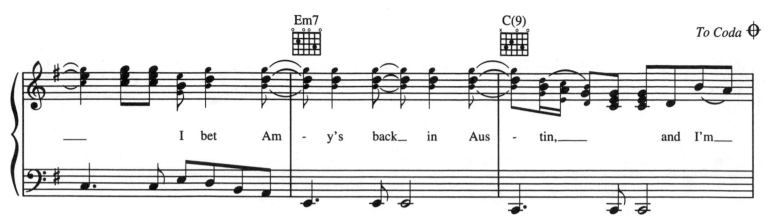

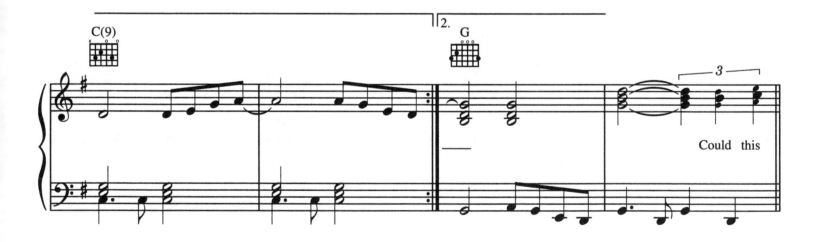

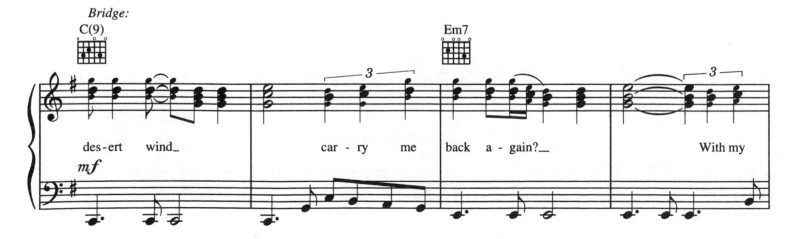

heart in my hand,___ ba - by, ba - by,_ I'm___ miss-ing you.___

miss-ing her,_____ miss - ing her___ to - night.___

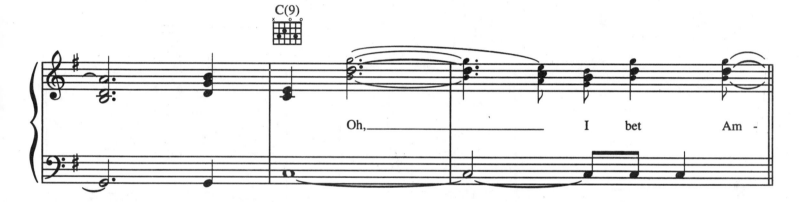

Oh,_____ I bet Am-

Repeat ad lib. and fade

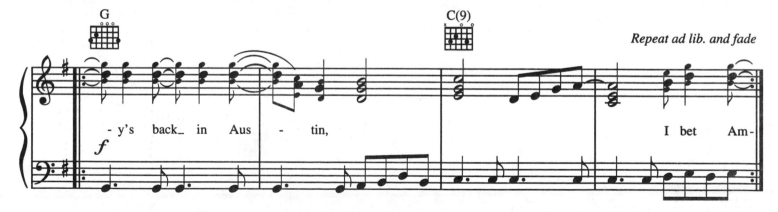

- y's back_ in Aus - tin, I bet Am-

Verse 2:
Workin' ten hours in a West Coast sun,
Can make the day so long.
Watchin' the moon crashin' into the ocean
Alone sure gets old.
I remember how sweet it was,
And where is she now, I need to know.
(To Chorus:)

I LOVE THE WAY YOU LOVE ME

Words and Music by
VICTORIA SHAW and
CHUCK CANNON

I Love the Way You Love Me - 4 - 1

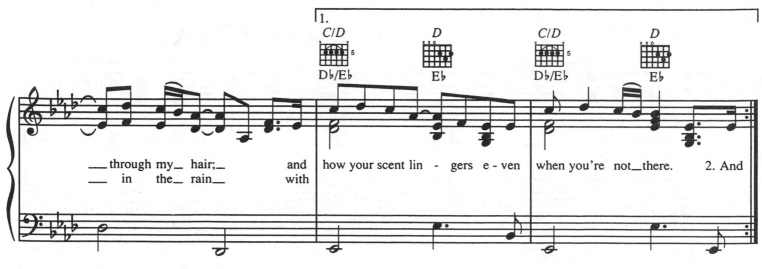

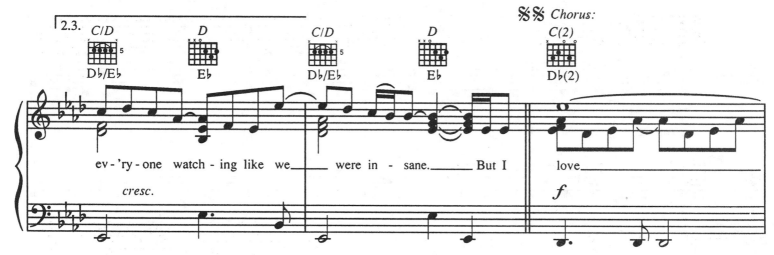

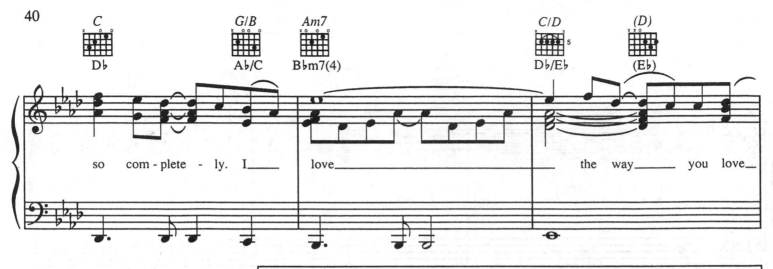

so com-plete-ly. I____ love_____ the way____ you love__

To Coda ⊕ | 1.   *D.S.* 𝄋

__ me.__

| 2.   *Bridge:*

And I could list__ a mil - lion things_

I love to like a - bout___ you,   but they all come_ down to__

D.S.S. 𝄋 𝄋 al Coda

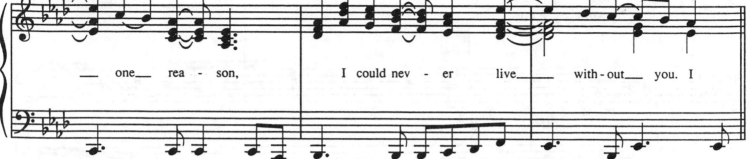

one___ rea - son,   I could nev - er   live___   with-out___ you. I

Oh ba - by, I___ love___   the way___ you love___

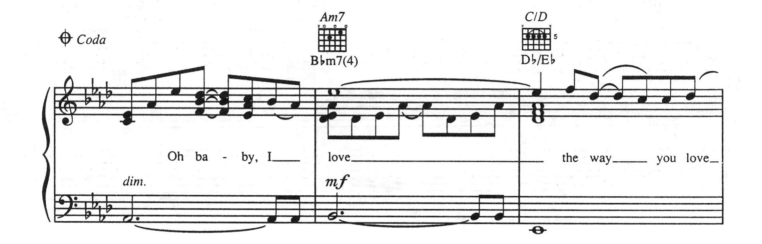

___ me.___

Verse 3:
I like to imitate ol' Jerry Lee
While you roll your eyes when I'm slightly off key.
And I like the innocent way that you cry
At sappy, old movies you've seen hundreds of times.
(To Chorus:)

NOT A MOMENT TOO SOON

Words and Music by
WAYNE PERRY and
JOE BARNHILL

1. I was stand-ing___ at the end of___ my

rain-bow,___ but no-where to go___ and no___ heart of gold___ in sight.

Not a Moment Too Soon - 4 - 1

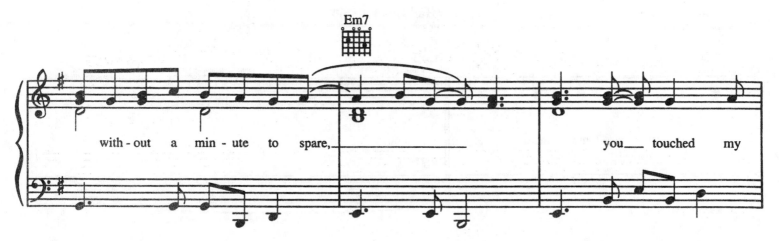

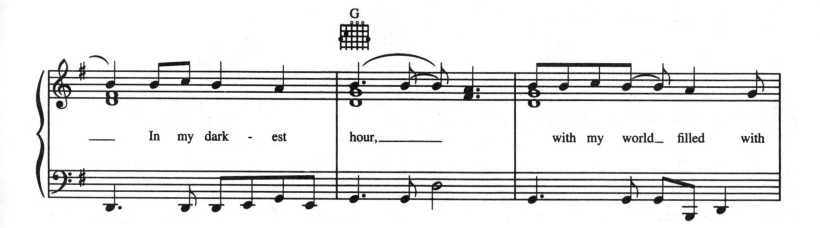

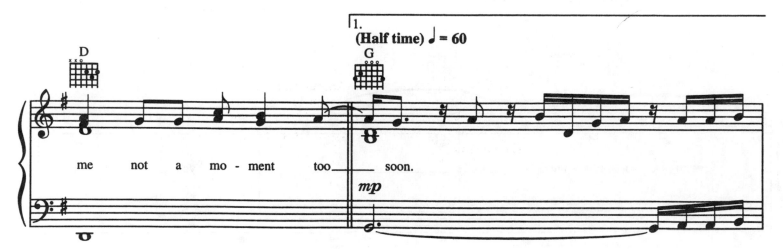

D.S. %

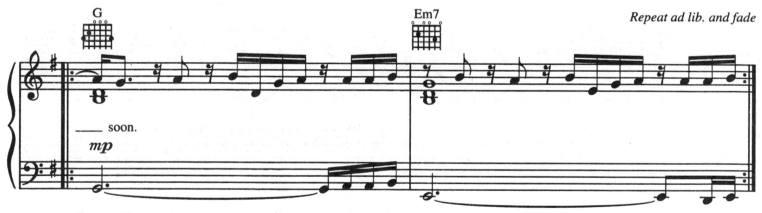

(Half time) ♩ = 60

Repeat ad lib. and fade

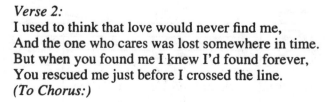

Verse 2:
I used to think that love would never find me,
And the one who cares was lost somewhere in time.
But when you found me I knew I'd found forever,
You rescued me just before I crossed the line.
(To Chorus:)

AS ANY FOOL CAN SEE

Words and Music by
KENNY BEARD and
PAUL NELSON

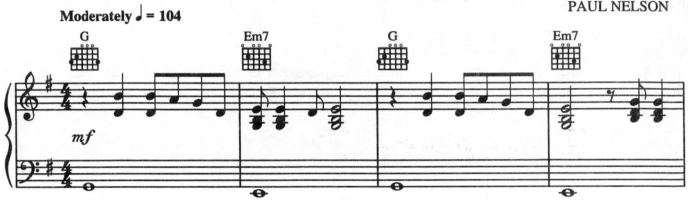

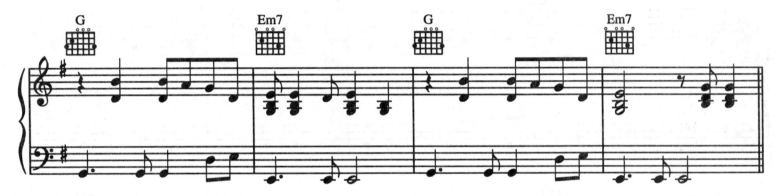

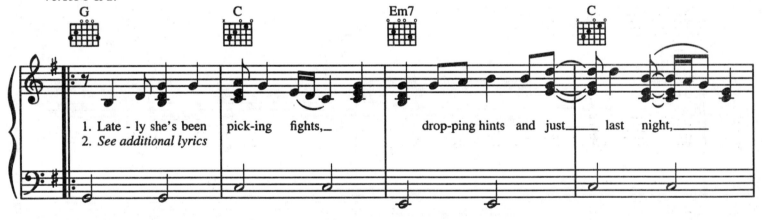

As Any Fool Can See - 4 - 1

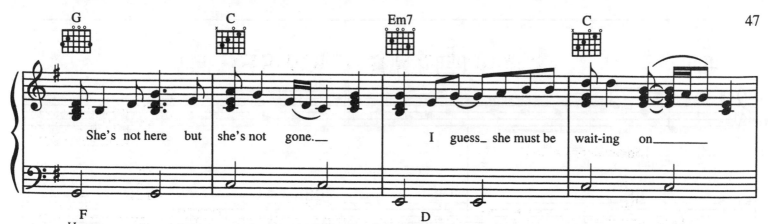

She's not here but she's not gone.___ I guess_ she must be wait-ing on___

the kind of man I prom-ised her___ I'd be.___ As an-y fool___ can see,___

Chorus:

___ she's gon-na cross that line,___ she's got leav-ing on___

___ her mind.___ And it's too late,___ but what keeps kill - ing me___

___ is know-ing I've been blind,___

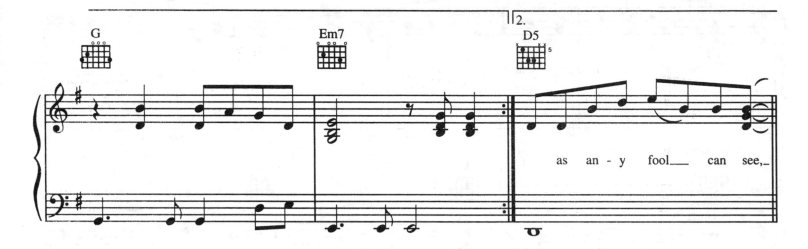

is know-ing I've been blind,___

as an-y fool___ can see,___ as an-y fool___ can see.___

Verse 2:
How long did I think she'd stand
For me to be the kind of man
That came and went just as I dang well pleased,
While she sits at home alone
With fears and feelings of her own?
Lord knows goodbye would bring me to my knees.
(To Chorus:)

BE MY BABY TONIGHT

Rock ♩ = 168

Words and Music by
ED HILL and RICH FAGAN

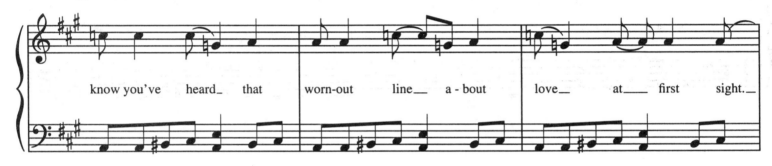

Be My Baby Tonight - 4 - 1

one look_____ to knock me off of my feet._____ I'm

not a man__ of man-y words,_ so I'll make this short_ and sweet._

Could you, would you, ain't you gon-na,

if I ask you, would you wan-na be my ba-by to-night?___ Yeah, I'll

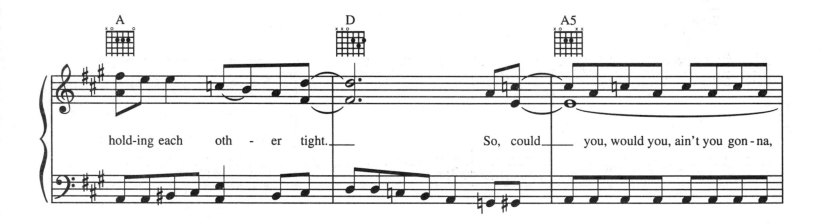

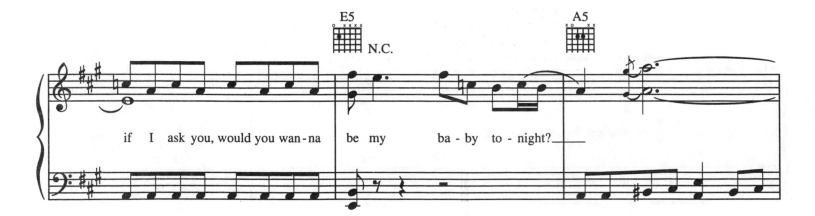

Well, could you, would you, ain't you gon-na, if I ask you, would you wan-na

be my ba - by to - night?_____

Verse 2:
I'm not trying to come on like some rhinestone Romeo.
I'm looking for a whole lot more than a one night rodeo.
What can I do to prove to you I'm laying it on the line?
I'll even get down on my knees just to beg you one more time.
(To Chorus:)

BLUE EYES CRYING IN THE RAIN

Words and Music by
FRED ROSE

Blue Eyes Crying In The Rain - 2 - 1

Blue Eyes Crying In The Rain - 2 - 2

THE BOX

Words and Music by
RANDY TRAVIS and BUCK MOORE

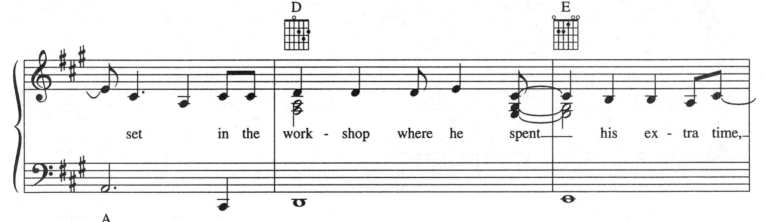

The Box - 6 - 1

The Box - 6 - 2

There was a let - ter____ from ma-

ma____ when she went out to Re - no____ to

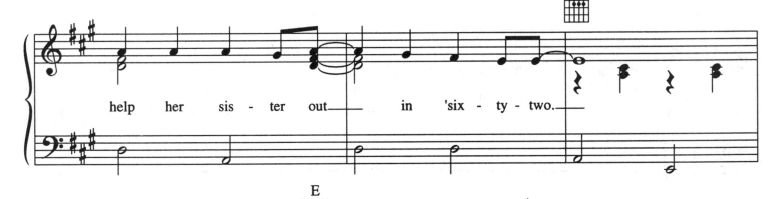

help her sis - ter out____ in 'six - ty - two.____

And a flo - wer from____ Haw - ai - i; when

they went on____ va - ca - tion, it was the first time that my

dad - dy ev - er flew. And the

pock - et knife__ I gave____ to him on Fa - ther's

Day;____ years a - go__ I thought__ it had been

lost. We all thought his heart was made__

__ of so - lid rock, but

The Box - 6 - 4

that was long__ be - fore__ we found__ the box.

I

box. We all thought his heart was made__

__ of sol - id rock, but

that was long__ be - fore__ we found__ the box.

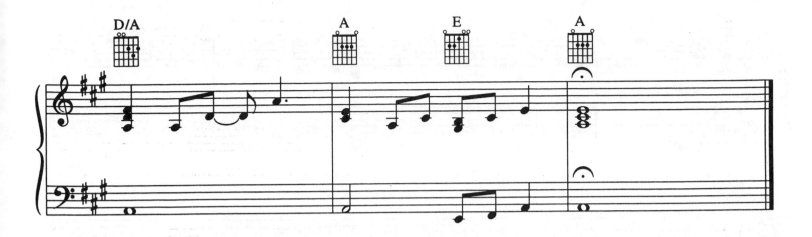

Additional lyrics

2. I guess we always knew it,
   But "I love you" was hard for him to say.
   Some men show it easily,
   And some just never seem to find the way.
   But that night I began to see
   A softer side of someone I had lost.
   I saw the love he kept inside the first time,
   When we opened up the box.

2nd Chorus: There was a picture that was taken,
   When he and mom were dating
   Standing by his 1944.
   And a faded leather bible
   He got when he was baptized,
   I guess no one understood him like the Lord.
   And a poem that he had written
   All about his wife and children,
   The tender words he wrote were quite a shock.
   We all thought his heart was made of solid rock,
   But that was long before we found the box.

COAT OF MANY COLORS

Words and Music by
DOLLY PARTON

1. Back through the years I go wan-d'ring once a-gain

back to the sea-sons of my youth. _____ I re-

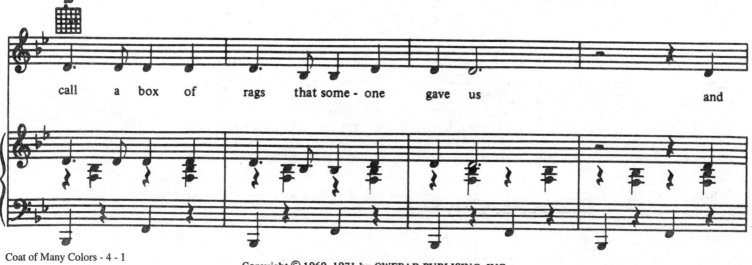

call a box of rags that some-one gave us and

Coat of Many Colors - 4 - 1

DON'T IT MAKE MY BROWN EYES BLUE

Words and Music by
RICHARD LEIGH

Don't It Make My Brown Eyes Blue - 2 - 1

DON'T TAKE THE GIRL

Words and Music by
CRAIG MARTIN and
LARRY W. JOHNSON

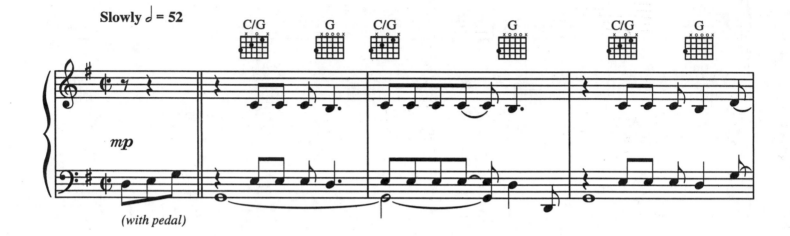

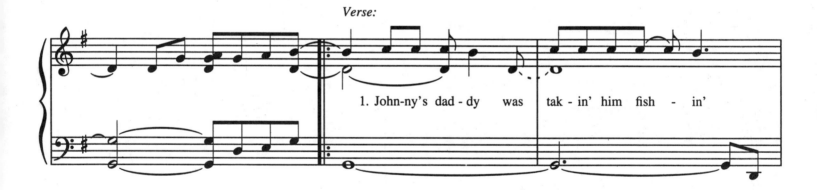

Don't Take the Girl - 4 - 1

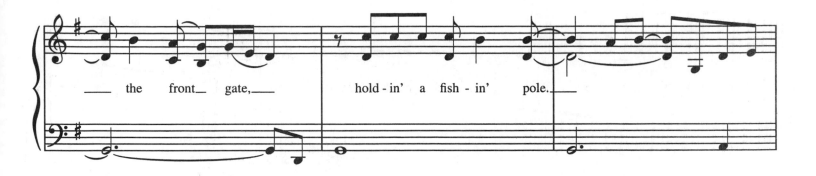

the front gate, hold-in' a fish-in' pole.

His dad looked down and smiled, said, "We can't leave her be - hind.

Son, I know you don't want her to go, but

some-day you'll change your mind." And John - ny said, "Take Jim - my John - son,

Don't Take the Girl - 4 - 2

take Tom-my Tomp - son, take my best friend, Bo.

Take an - y - bod - y that you want as long as she don't go.

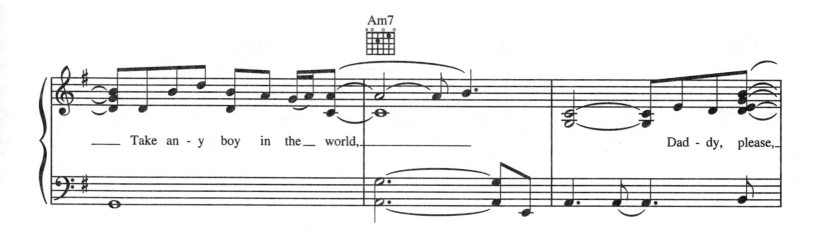

Take an - y boy in the world, Dad - dy, please,

don't take the girl."

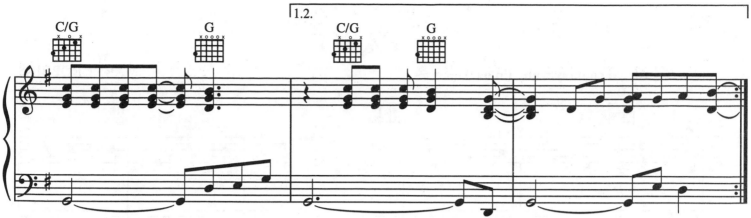

Verse 2:
Same ol' boy, same sweet girl, ten years down the road.
He held her tight and kissed her lips in front of the picture show.
A stranger came and pulled a gun and grabbed her by the arm.
Said, "If you do what I tell you to, there won't be any harm."
And Johnny said,
"Take my money, take my wallet, take my credit cards.
Here's the watch that my grandpa gave me, here's the keys to my car.
Mr., give it a whirl, but please, don't take the girl."

Verse 3:
Same ol' boy, same sweet girl, five years down the road.
There's gonna be a little one and she says, "It's time to go."
Doctor said, "The baby's fine but, you'll have to leave
'Cause his mama's fadin' fast," and Johnny hit his knees.
And then he prayed,
"Take the very breath you gave me, take the heart from my chest.
I'll gladly take her place if you'll have me.
Make this my last request.
Take me out of this world, God, please, don't take the girl."

EL PASO

Written by
MARTY ROBBINS

Bright country waltz (in one) ♩. = 69

𝄋 *Verse 1 - 11:*

1. Out in the west Tex-as town of El Pas-o,
2. Night-time would find me in Rose-'s Can-ti-na,
3. Black-er than night were the eyes of Fe-li-na,
4. My love was deep for this Mex-i-can maid-en,

I fell in love with a Mex-i-can girl. _____
mu-sic would play and Fe-li-na would whirl. _____
wick-ed and e-vil while cast-ing a spell. _____
I was in love, but in vain, I could tell. _____

El Paso - 6 - 1

Bridge:

1. One night a wild young cow-boy came in, wild as the
2. Out through the back door of Rose-'s I ran, out where the
3. I sad-dle up and a-way I did go, rid-ing a-
4. Some-thing is dread-ful-ly wrong, for I feel a deep burn-ing

west Tex-as wind.
hors-es were tied.
lone in the dark.
pain in my side.

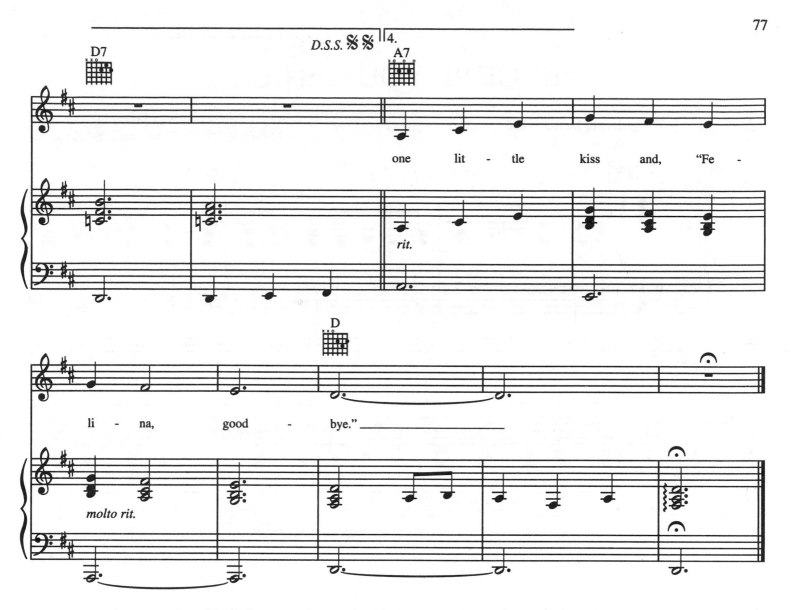

Verse 5:
So, in anger, I challenged his right for the love of this maiden.
Down went his hand for the gun that he wore.

Verse 6:
My challenge was answered, in less than a heartbeat,
The handsome young stranger lay dead on the floor.

Verse 7:
Just for a moment I stood there in silence,
Shocked by the foul, evil deed I had done.

Verse 8:
Many thoughts raced through my mind as I stood there.
I had but one chance and that was to run.
(To Bridge 2:)

Verse 9:
. . . Just as fast as I could from the west Texas town of El Paso
Out to the badlands of New Mexico.

Verse 10:
Back in El Paso, my life would be worthless.
Everything's gone in life, nothing is left.

Verse 11:
It's been so long since I've seen the young maiden,
My love is stronger than my fear of death.
(To Bridge 3:)

EUGENE YOU GENIUS

Words and Music by
LONNIE WILSON and BILLY LAWSON

Moderate beat ♩ = 120

1. Saw___ you come through them___
2. *See additional lyrics.*

swing-ing doors,___ had___ 'em hang-ing on ya, could-n't hold one more.

Eugene You Genius - 4 - 1

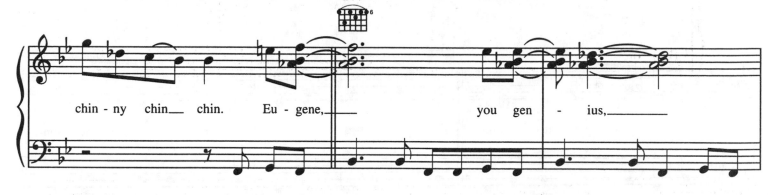

You walked by____ with a sil-ly grin,____ they were kiss-ing all o-ver your

chin-ny chin__ chin. Eu-gene,____ you gen - ius,____

what book did you read____ that made__ you so smart,

you could steal a heart an-y-time that you please?____ Eu - gene,__

____ you gen - ius,_____ could you teach

- ius. _____

(Inst. solo . . .

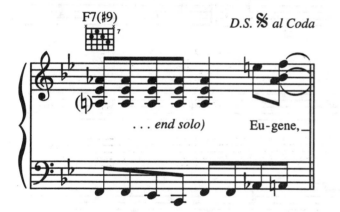

. . . end solo) Eu-gene, ___

me? Eu-gene, ___

you gen - ius. Eu-gene, ___

Verse 2:
It's more than the way you comb your hair,
That's making all the pretty girls stop and stare.
Tell me Eugene, I just gotta know,
Can I go down and buy it at the grocery store?
(To Chorus:)

A GOOD HEARTED WOMAN

Words and Music by
WILLIE NELSON and WAYLON JENNINGS

A Good Hearted Woman - 4 - 1

A Good Hearted Woman - 4 - 3

Through tear - drops and laugh - ter, they'll

pass through this world — hand - in - hand,

a good - heart - ed wo - man lov - in' her good - tim - in'

man. She's a

A Good Hearted Woman - 4 - 4

THE HEART IS A LONELY HUNTER

Words and Music by
MARK D. SANDERS, KIM WILLIAMS
and ED HILL

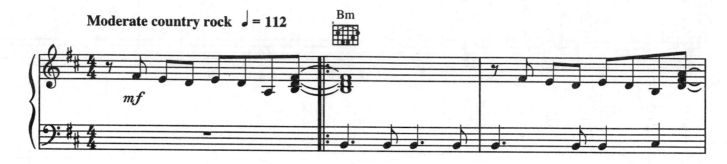

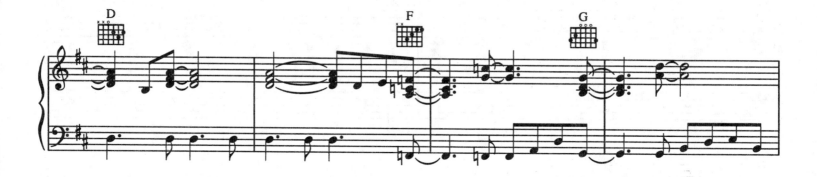

1. She came in look-in' good___ and look-in' a -
2. She hears him say, "Hey, can___ I buy you a

The Heart Is a Lonely Hunter - 6 - 1

90

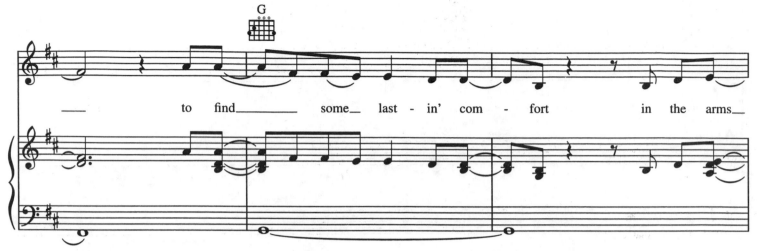

to find_____ some___ last - in' com - fort in the arms___

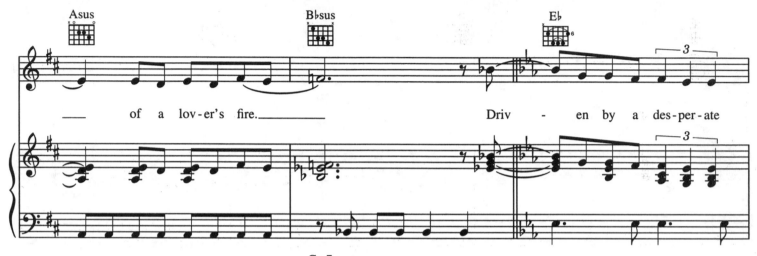

_____ of a lov - er's fire._____ Driv - en by a des - per - ate

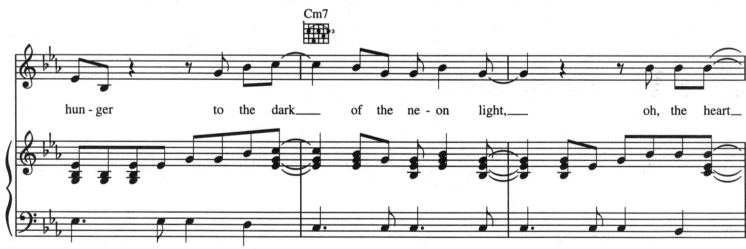

hun - ger to the dark___ of the ne - on light,___ oh, the heart___

_____ is a lone - ly hunt - er when there's no sign of___ love in___

The Heart Is a Lonely Hunter - 6 - 5

sight.   Oh, the heart_____ is a lone - ly hunt - er   when there's no

sign of   love in sight.

I'LL STILL BE LOVING YOU

Words and Music by
PAT BUNCH, PAM ROSE,
MARY ANN KENNEDY and TODD CERNEY

HEY, GOOD LOOKIN'

Words and Music by
HANK WILLIAMS

Hey, Good Lookin' - 2 - 1

Hey, Good Lookin' - 2 - 2

I AM WHO I AM

Words and Music by
TOM SHAPIRO, CHRIS WATERS
and HOLLY DUNN

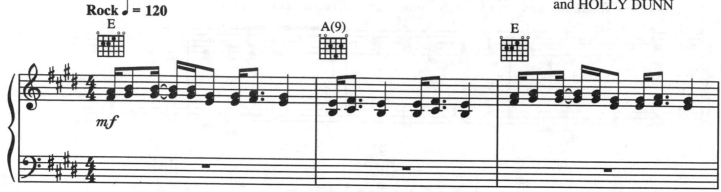

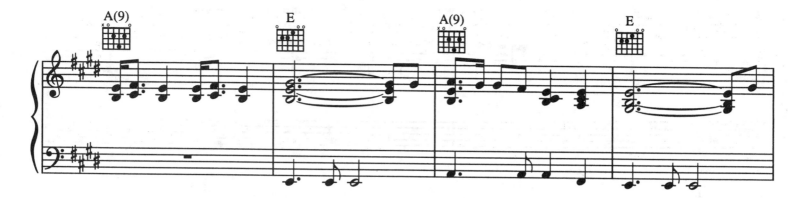

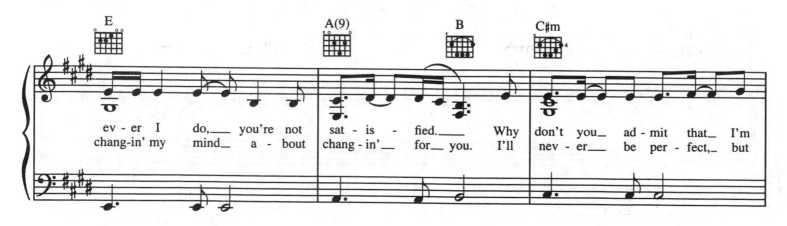

I Am Who I Am - 4 - 1

not what_ you need,___ so I can_ find some-one_ who'll love me_ for me?_ }
I'll be_ al-right___ now that_ I've start-ed to live my_ own life._ I

% *Chorus:*

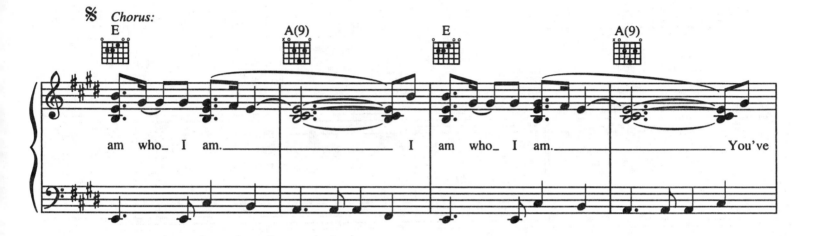

am who_ I am.___ I am who_ I am.___ You've

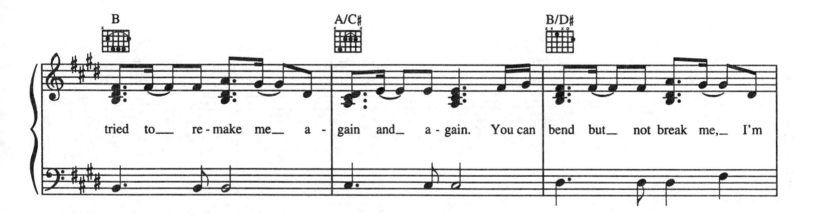

tried to_ re-make me_ a-gain and_ a-gain. You can bend but_ not break me,_ I'm

To Coda ⊕ | 1.

tak-in'_ a stand. { You get what_ you see, ba-by._ I am who_ I
I'm all I_ can be, ba-by._ am._

I Am Who I Am - 4 - 2

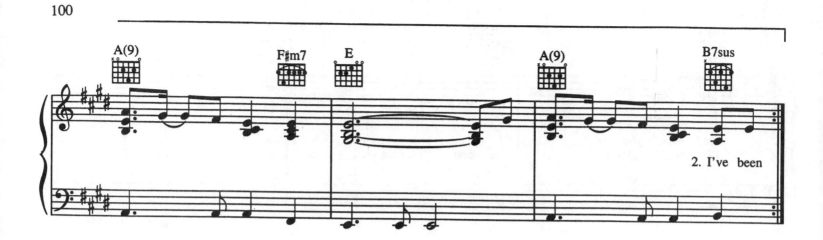

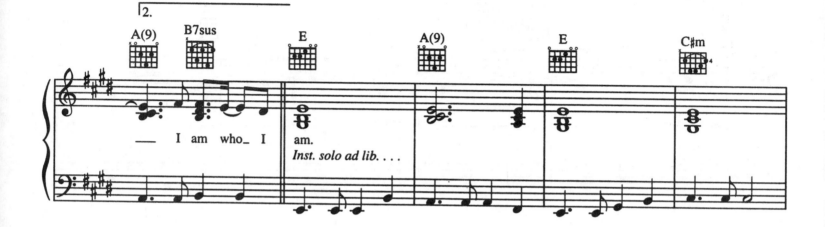

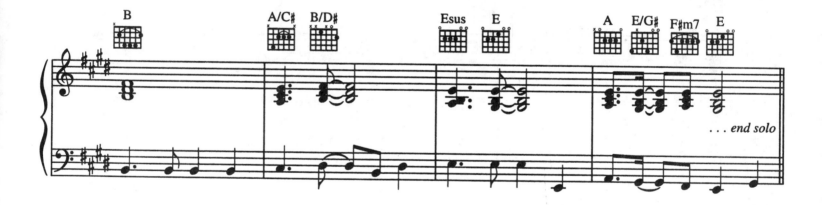

D.S. 𝄋 al Coda

can't be___ right for___ you if___ it's not right___ for___ me.___ I

⊕ Coda

___ I am who___ I am. I'm

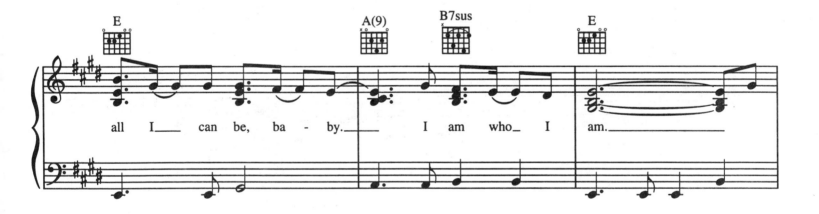

all I___ can be, ba-by.___ I am who___ I am.___

I am who___ I am.___

I CROSS MY HEART

Words and Music by
STEVE DORFF and
ERIC KAZ

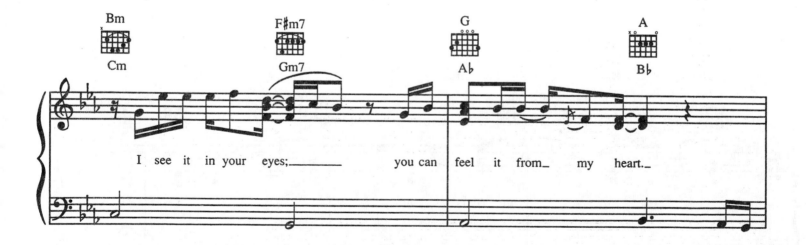

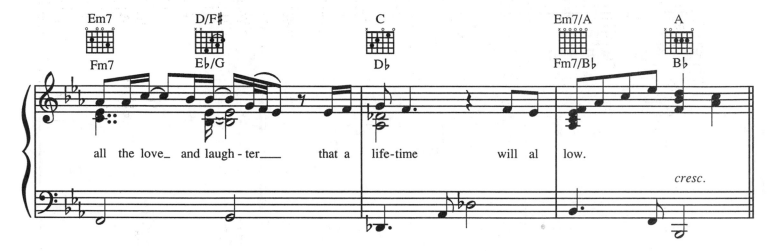

Chorus:

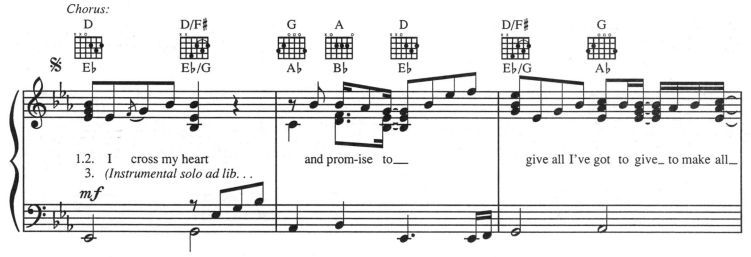

I Cross My Heart - 4 - 2

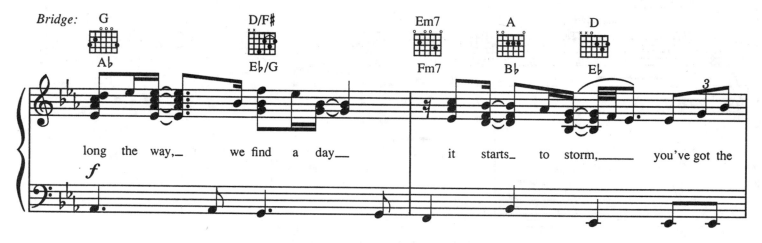

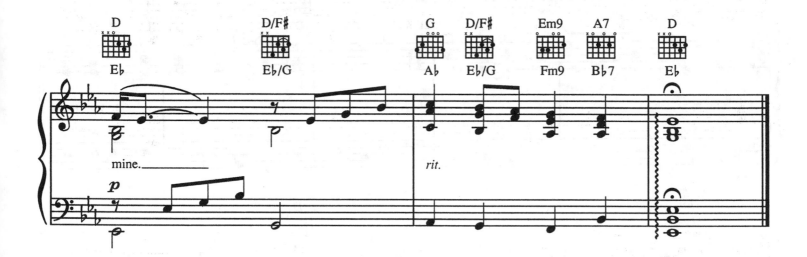

Verse 2:
You will always be the miracle
That makes my life complete;
And as long as there's a breath in me,
I'll make yours just as sweet.
As we look into the future,
It's as far as we can see,
So let's make each tomorrow
Be the best that it can be.
(To Chorus:)

I DIDN'T KNOW MY OWN STRENGTH

Words and Music by
RICK BOWLES and ROBERT BYRNE

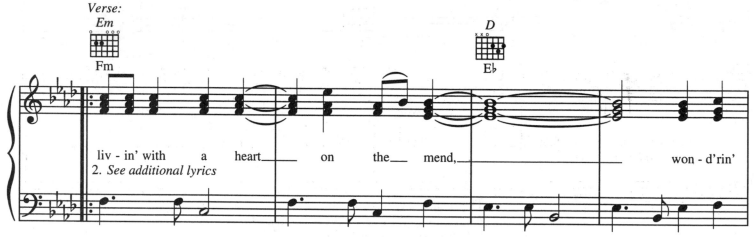

I Didn't Know My Own Strength - 4 - 1

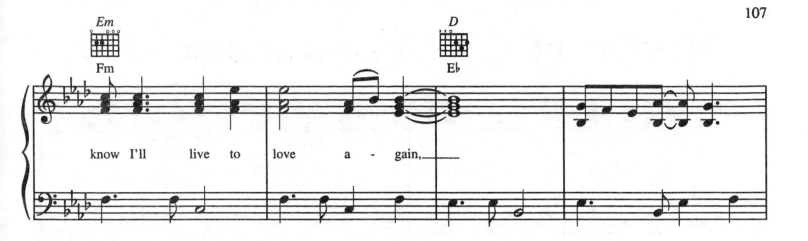

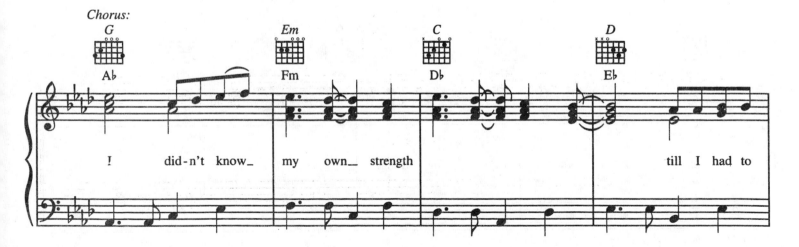

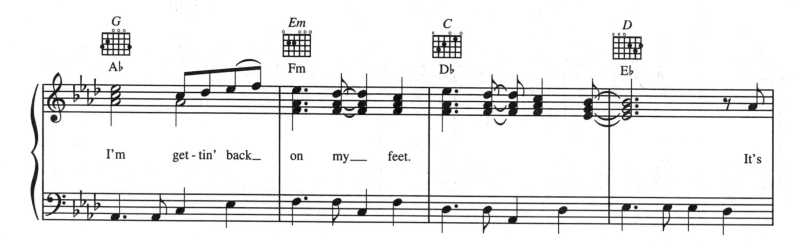

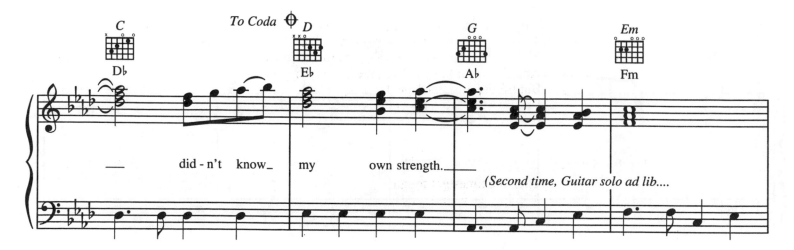

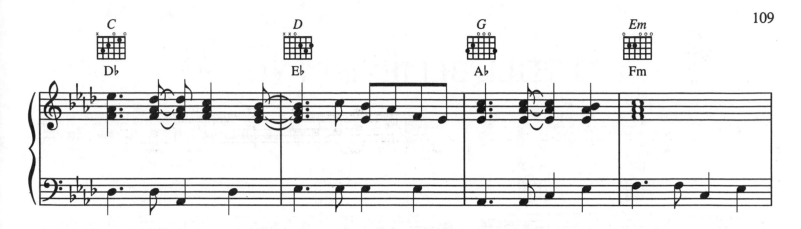

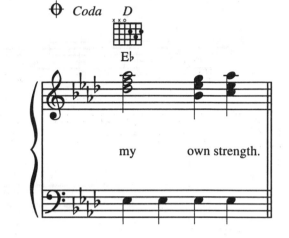

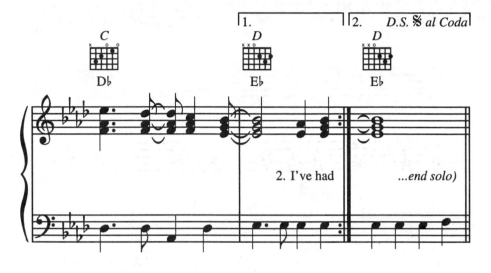

Verse 2:
I've had oceans of tears to get through
And the weight of the world on my mind.
There've been mountains of memories to move
And I've been beating back the blows to my pride.
But till the times got tough,
I never knew what I was made of.
(To Chorus:)

Verse 3:
Then the times got tough
And I knew what I was made of.
(To Chorus:)

I STILL BELIEVE IN YOU

Words and Music by
VINCE GILL and JOHN BARLOW JARVIS

to see the tears you cry____ fall - in'____ like rain._____ Give me the chance____

____ to prove_____ and I'll make it up to____ you.

cresc.

Chorus:

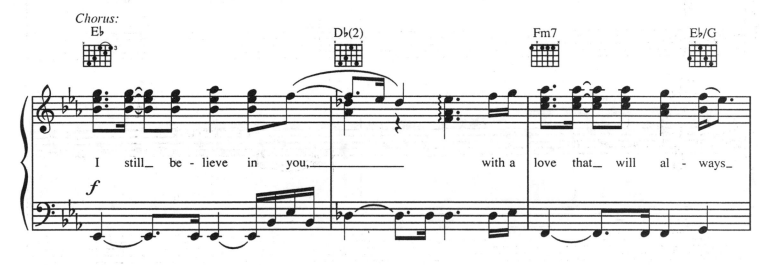

I still____ be - lieve in you,_____ with a love that____ will al - ways____

f

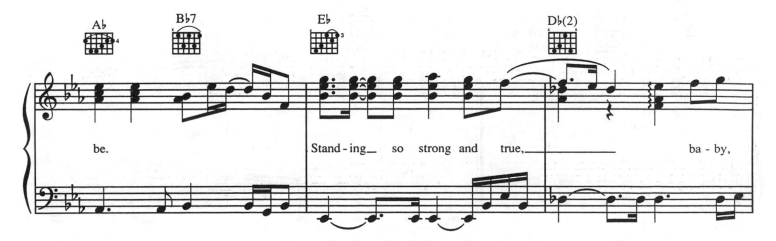

be. Stand - ing____ so strong and true,_____ ba - by,

I still be-lieve in you and me.

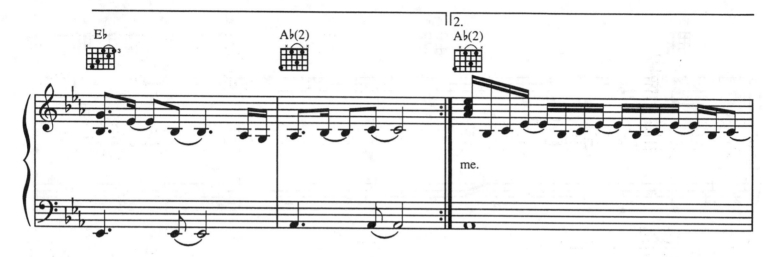

me.

Ba-by, I still be-lieve in you, with a

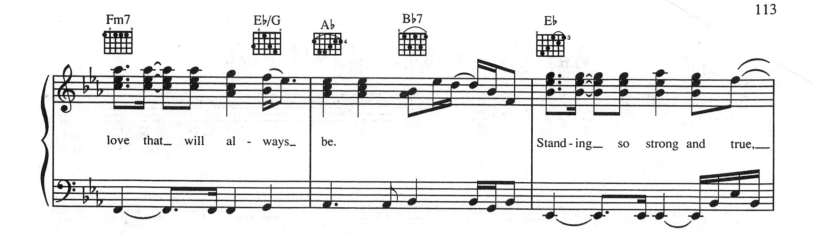

love that_ will al - ways_ be. Stand-ing_ so strong and true,_

_ ba-by, I still_ be - lieve in_ you. Ba-by, you_ and

me. *rit.*

Verse 2:
Somewhere along the way, I guess I just lost track,
Only thinkin' of myself, never lookin' back.
For all the times I've hurt you, I apologize,
I'm sorry it took so long to finally realize.
Give me the chance to prove
That nothing's worth losing you.
(To Chorus:)

I WILL ALWAYS LOVE YOU

Words and Music by
DOLLY PARTON

Slow

If

I should___ stay; well, I would on-ly be in___ your

2.3.*(See additional lyrics)*

way,_____ and so I'll go, and yet I know that I'll think

I Will Always Love You - 2 - 1

Chorus

of you each step___ of my way,_____ and I _____ will
al - ways __ love __ you; ___ I ___ will al - ways __ love __
you.
you. *I will always love you.*
2. Bit - ter

Verse 2:
Bitter sweet memories, that's all I have and all I'm taking with me.
Good-bye, oh please don't cry, 'cause we both know that I'm not what you need, but . . .
(To Chorus:)

Verse 3: (Recite)
And I hope life will treat you kind, and I hope that you have all that you ever dreamed of.
Oh, I do wish you joy, and I wish you happiness, but above all this, I wish you love;
I love you, I will always love you. (To Chorus:)

IF I EVER FALL IN LOVE AGAIN

Words by
GLORIA SKLEROV

Music by
STEVE DORFF

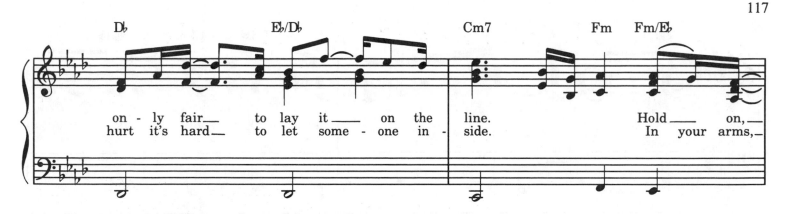

on-ly fair___ to lay it___ on the line. Hold___ on,___
hurt it's hard___ to let some-one in - side. In your arms,___

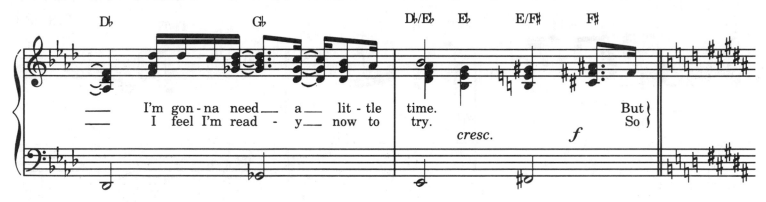

___ I'm gon-na need___ a___ lit-tle time. But
___ I feel I'm read - y___ now to try. So

cresc. *f*

Chorus:

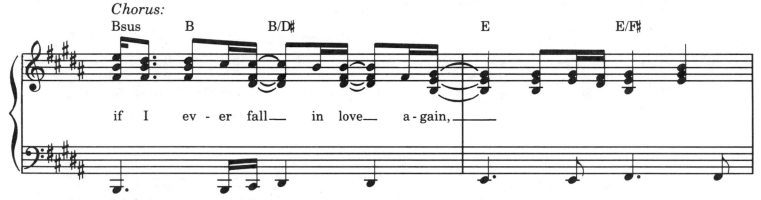

if I ev - er fall___ in love___ a-gain,___

some-time when this bro - ken heart can mend.___ I know it's

gon-na be___ with you.___ You're the one to pull___ me through,___ though I don't know when,

If I Ever Fall In Love Again - 4 - 2

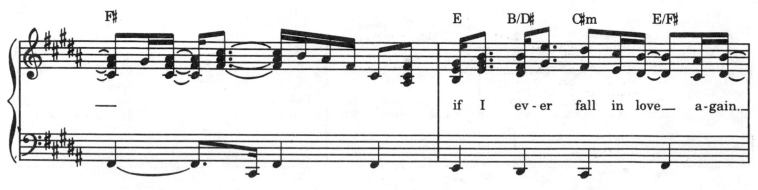

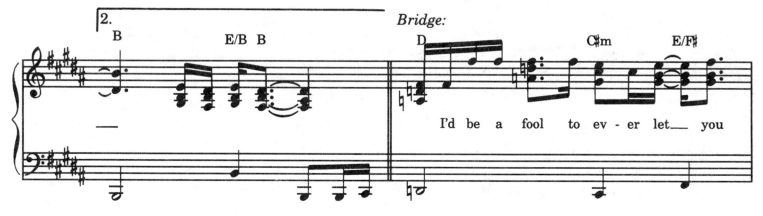

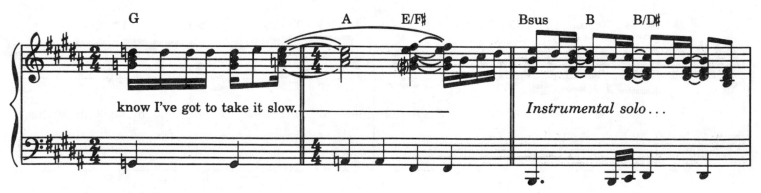

If I Ever Fall In Love Again - 4 - 4

IF YOU'VE GOT LOVE

Words and Music by
STEVE SESKIN and MARK SANDERS

Moderate country two-beat ♩ = 60

If You've Got Love - 4 - 1

noth - in' quite__ like life____ if you've____ got love._____

you've got love,__ you've____ got what__ it takes._____

If you've got

cresc.

Chorus:

love you can move__ a moun - tain a lit-tle bit fur-ther down__ the line.____ You can do it

f

all at once,____ or one rock at____ a time.____ You can turn an

or - di - nar - y pic - ture in - to a price-less work of art.____ That's what you can do__

1.

____ if you've__ got__ love__ in__ your__ heart. *dim.* *mf*

THE KEEPER OF THE STARS

Words and Music by
KAREN STALEY, DANNY MAYO and DICKEY LEE

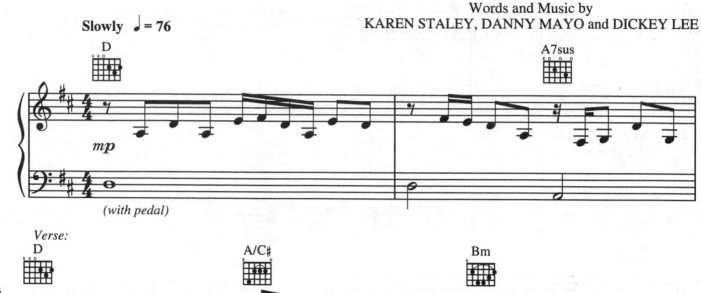

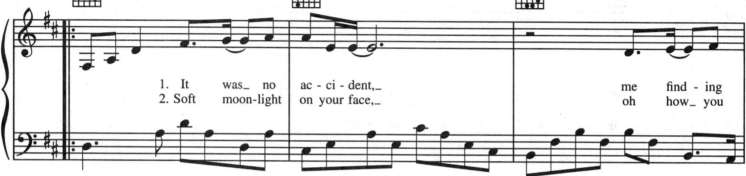

1. It was no ac-ci-dent,___ me find-ing
2. Soft moon-light on your face,___ oh how_ you

you. Some-one had a hand_ in it___
shine! It takes my_ breath_ a-way___

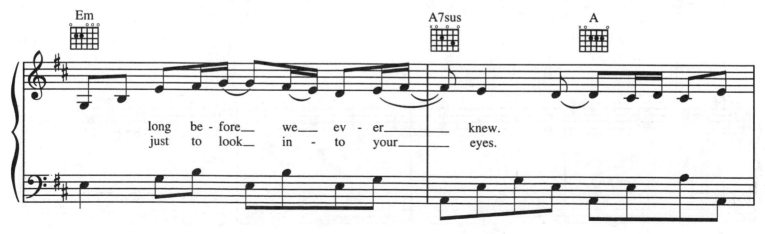

long be-fore_ we_ ev-er___ knew.
just to look_ in-to your___ eyes.

The Keeper of the Stars - 4 - 1

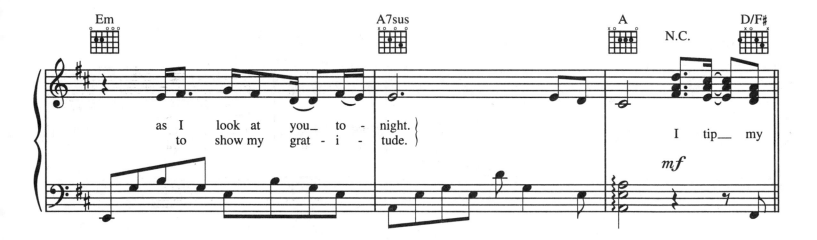

The Keeper of the Stars - 4 - 2

He sure knew what he___ was do - in'___ when he joined these two__

hearts. I hold ev - 'ry - thing

when I hold you in my_ arms. I've got all I'll ev-er need

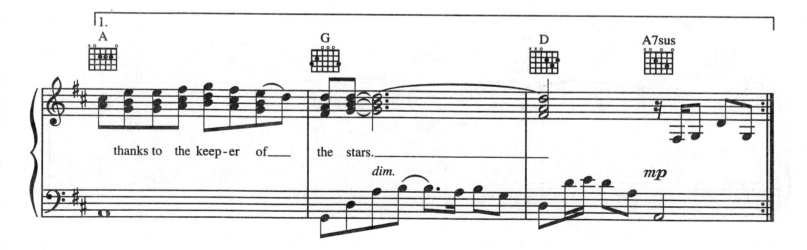

thanks to the keep-er of___ the stars.___

dim.

mp

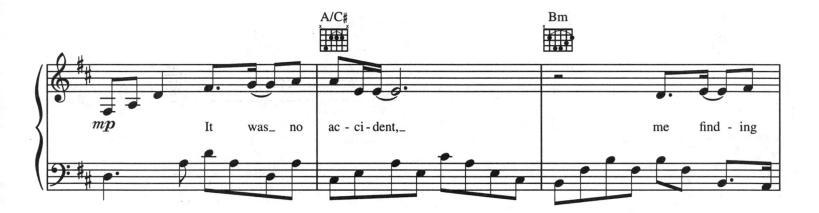

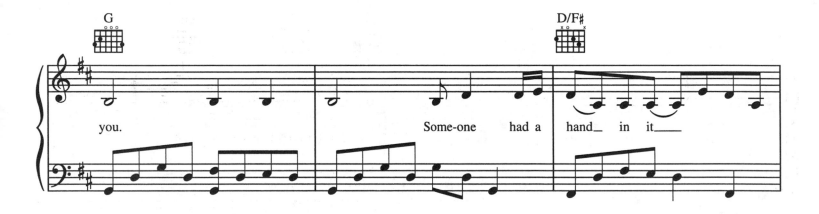

The Keeper of the Stars - 4 - 4

LIVIN' ON LOVE

Words and Music by
ALAN JACKSON

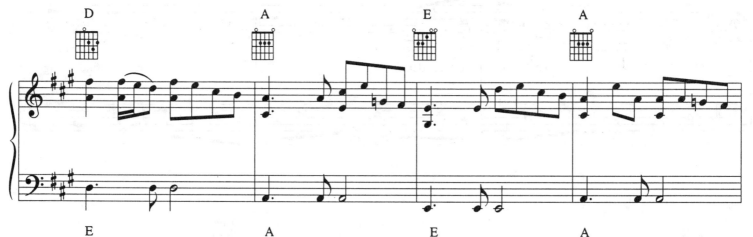

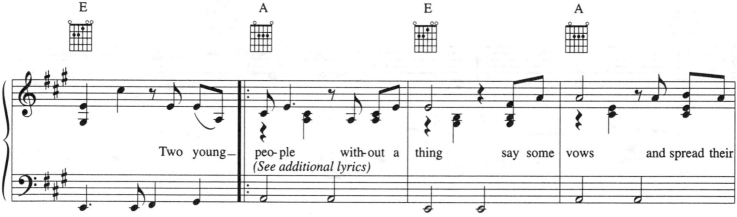

Livin' on Love - 4 - 1

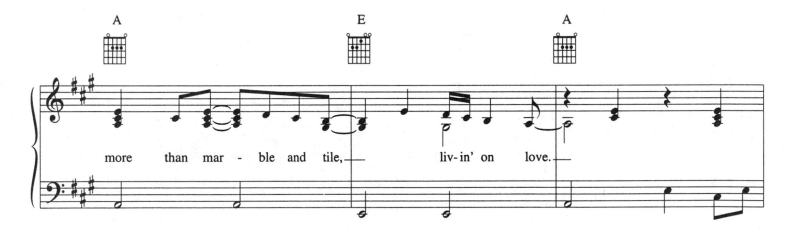

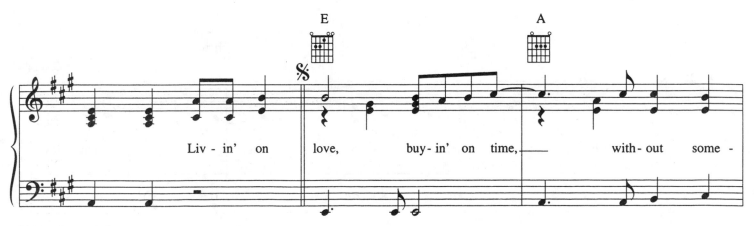

Livin' on Love - 4 - 2

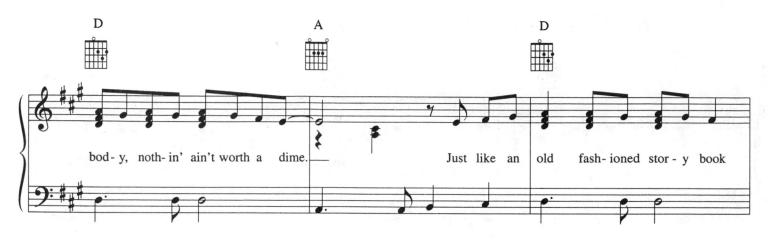

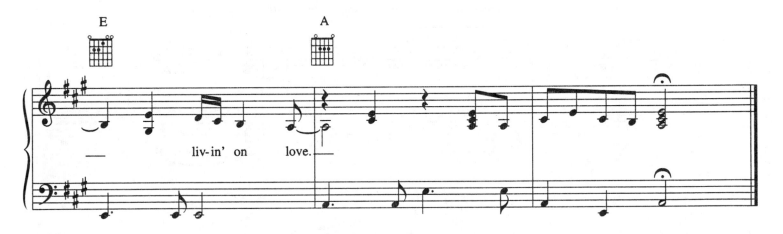

Additional Lyrics

2. Two old people without a thing
   Children gone but still they sing
   Side by side in that front porch swing
   Livin' on love.
   He can't see anymore,
   She can barely sweep the floor.
   Hand in hand they'll walk through that door
   Just livin' on love.
   (To Chorus)

LOVE IN THE FIRST DEGREE

Words and Music by
JIM HURT and TIM DuBOIS

Love in the First Degree - 4 - 1

Love in the First Degree - 4 - 2

Love in the First Degree - 4 - 4

OH, LONESOME ME

Words and Music by
DON GIBSON

Oh, Lonesome Me - 4 - 1

-in' none. _____ I can't get o - ver how _____

_____ she set _____ me free. _____

Oh, _____ lone - some me. _____ 2. A bad _____

1. Well, I'll bet _____ she's not _____ like me, _____ she's out _____ and fan - cy free. _____

Flirt - ing with the boys with all her charms.

But, I here in my arms. Well, there must

be some - way I can lose these lone - some blues. For-

get a - bout the past and find some - bod-y new. I've

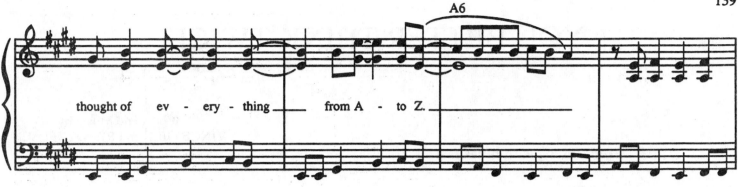

thought of ev - ery - thing ___ from A - to Z. ___

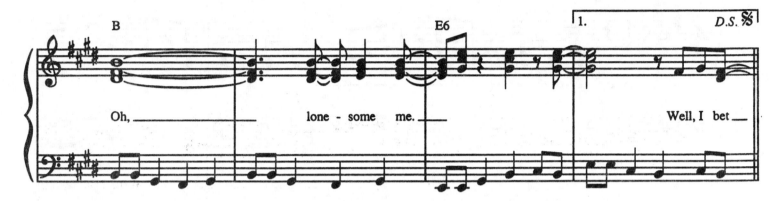

Oh, ___ lone - some me. ___ Well, I bet ___

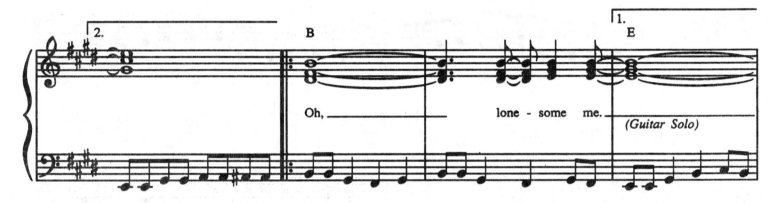

Oh, ___ lone - some me. ___ (Guitar Solo)

(Guitar Solo to end)

Verse 2:
A bad mistake I'm makin' by just hangin' 'round.
I know that I should have some fun and paint the town.
A love sick fool that's blind and just can't see.
Oh, lonesome me.

Bridges 2 & 4:
But, I still love her so.
And brother, don't you know,
I'd welcome her right back here in my arms.

YOU BETTER THINK TWICE

Words and Music by
VINCE GILL and REED NIELSEN

Moderately, with blues feel

I know—

it ain't none of my busi - ness *(See additional lyrics)* when it comes— to the af-fairs of your heart.—

— It's real - ly hard for me to say this,— but your trou-

You Better Think Twice - 4 - 1

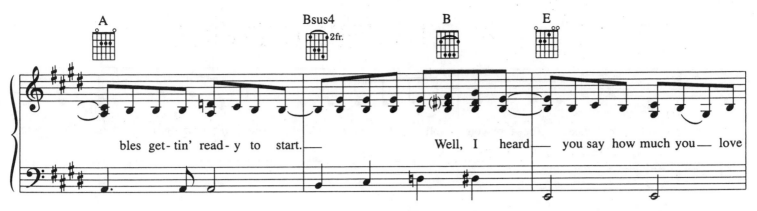

141

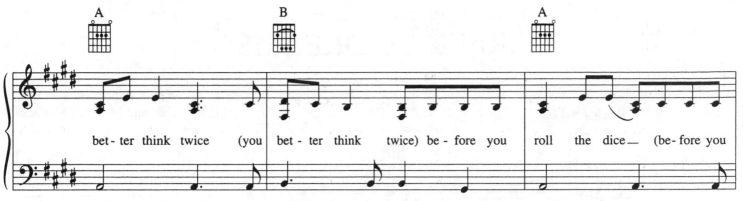

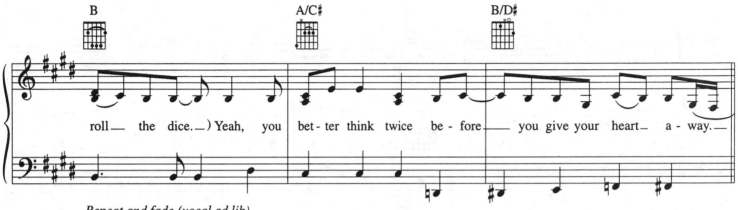

Repeat and fade (vocal ad lib)

Additional lyrics

2. You really must think I'm something,
   Talkin' trash about my best friend.
   I just hate to see you wind up with nothing,
   'Cause you're way too good for him.
   I know that you don't believe me,
   But I've been with him when he's runnin' 'round.
   He don't mean to hurt nobody,
   He ain't never gonna settle down.
   (To Chorus)

3. *Instrumental*
   (To Chorus)

REFRIED DREAMS

Words and Music by
JIM FOSTER and MARK PETERSEN

Refried Dreams - 4 - 1

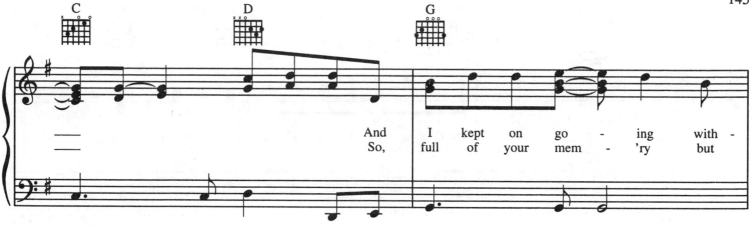

And I kept on go - ing with -
So, full of your mem - 'ry with but

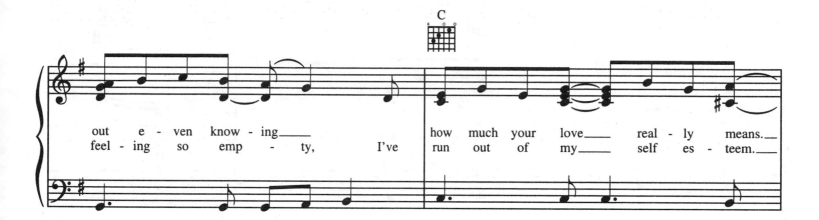

out e - ven know - ing___ how much your love___ real - ly means.___
feel - ing so emp - ty, I've run out of my___ self es - teem.___

Now, I'm messed up in Mex - i - co, liv - ing on re - fried

Chorus:

dreams.___ I'm down here in Mex - i - co,

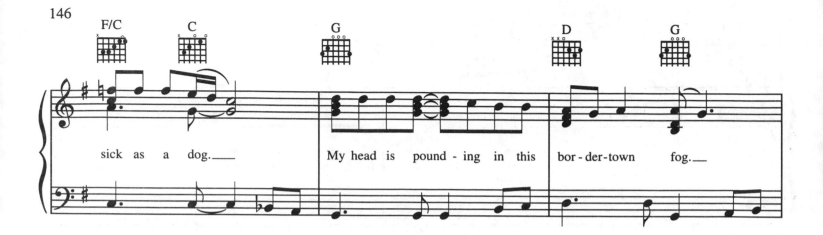

sick as a dog.___ My head is pound-ing in this bor-der-town fog.___

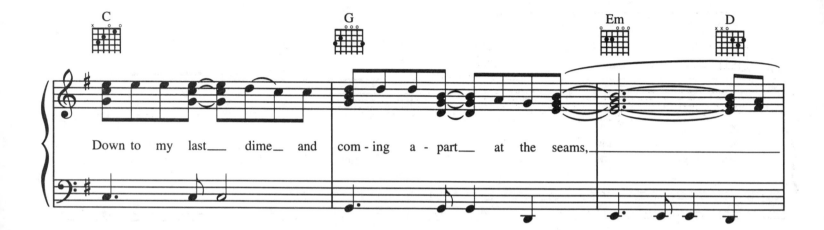

Down to my last___ dime___ and com-ing a-part___ at the seams,___

___ I'm messed up in Mex-i-co, liv-ing on re-fried

dreams._

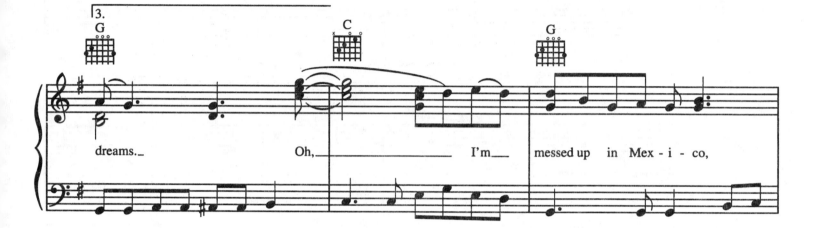

YOU CAN SLEEP WHILE I DRIVE

Lyrics and Music by
MELISSA ETHERIDGE

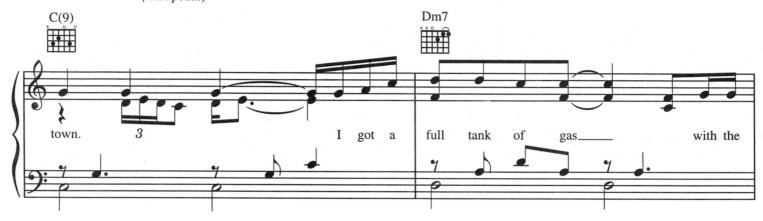

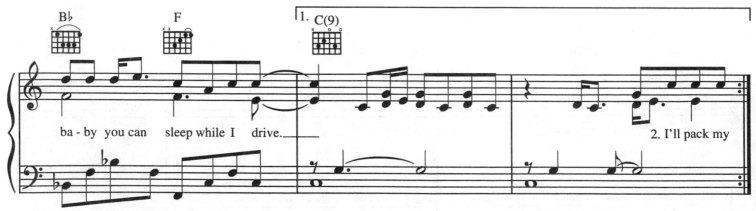

* Melody sung 1 octave lower

You Can Sleep While I Drive - 4 - 1

3. We'll go through   You know I've

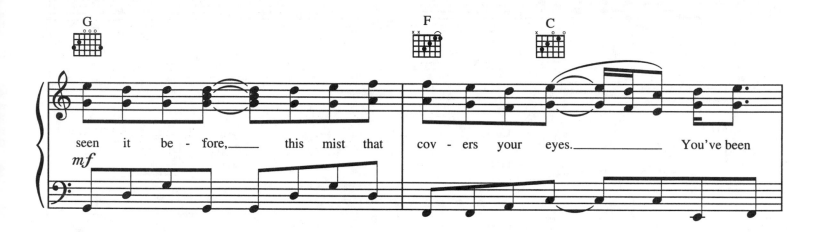

seen it be - fore,___ this mist that cov - ers your eyes.___ You've been

look-ing for some-thing that's not___ in your_ life. My in - ten-tions are true,___ won't you

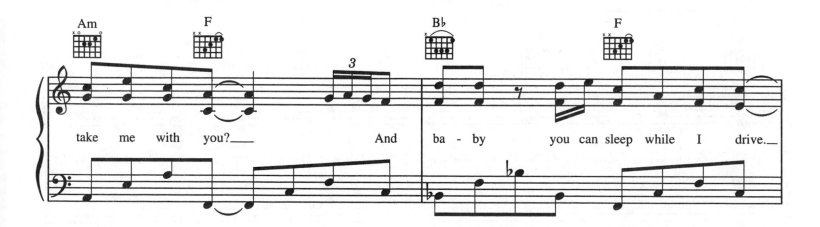

take me with you?___ And ba - by you can sleep while I drive.___

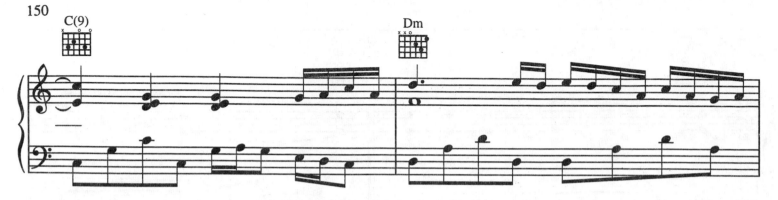

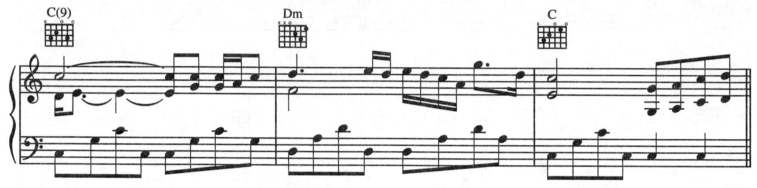

Oh_____ is it oth - er arms_ you want to hold_____

you,_____ the strang - er,_____ the lov - er, you're free.____ Can't you

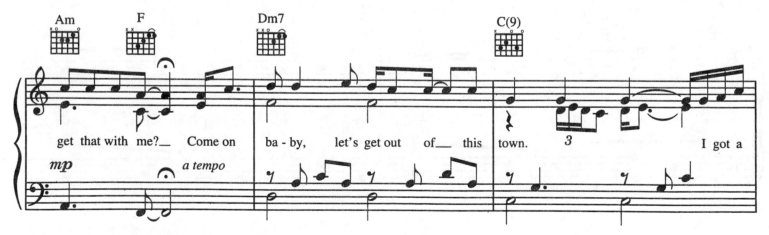

get that with me?__ Come on ba - by, let's get out of__ this town. I got a

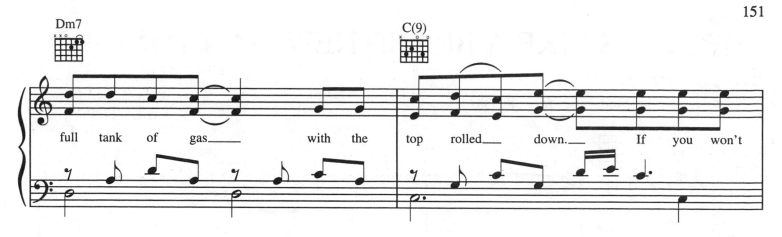

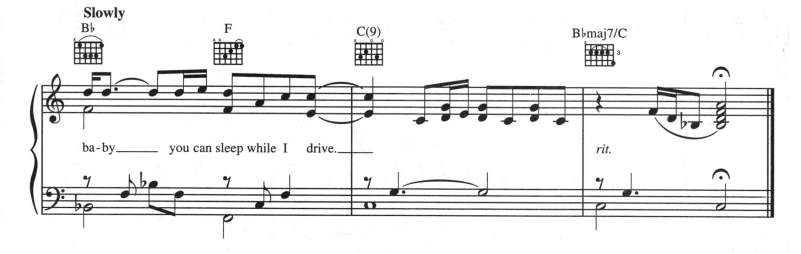

Verse 2:
I'll pack my bag and load up my guitar,
In my pocket I'll carry my harp.
I got some money I saved,
Enough to get underway,
And baby you can sleep while I drive.

Verse 3:
We'll go through Tucson up to Sante Fe,
And Barbara in Nashville says we're welcome to stay.
I'll buy you boots down in Texas,
A hat in New Orleans,
And in the morning you can tell me your dreams.

SHE FEELS LIKE A BRAND NEW MAN TONIGHT

Words and Music by
AARON TIPPIN and
MICHAEL P. HEENEY

Moderately fast ♩ = 138

1. Her last lonely tear-
2. See additional lyrics

drops fell along about nine o'clock. His

She Feels Like a Brand New Man Tonight - 4 - 1

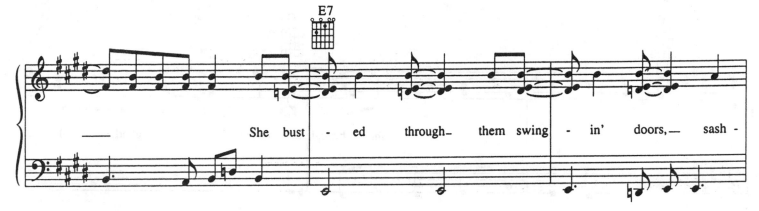

She did-n't come in here— to hang— her head and cry.—

— She's through— throw-in'— good— love—

— a way— on some boy that don't treat her right.—

She feels— like a brand— new— man— to-night.—

1.

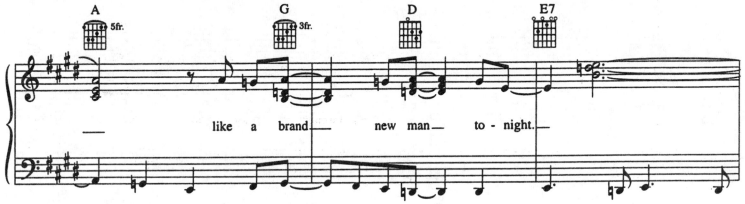

Verse 2:
Just like a kid in a candy store,
She's checking out the merchandise.
But she wants to find the keeping kind,
Who will keep her satisfied.
And he's gotta have a tender touch,
So if you fit the bill, brother, don't sit still.
Come on, step right up 'cause...
(To Chorus:)

SINGING THE BLUES

Words and Music by
MELVIN ENDSLEY

Singing The Blues - 2 - 1

SLOW HAND

Words and Music by
MICHAEL CLARK and JOHN BETTIS

Slow Hand - 4 - 1

SWEET DREAMS

Words and Music by
DON GIBSON

Sweet Dreams - 2 - 1

TAKE THESE CHAINS FROM MY HEART

Words and Music by
FRED ROSE and HY HEATH

Country shuffle ♩ = 132

1. Take these chains from my heart___ and set me free.
2. Take these tears from my eyes___ and let me see___

You've grown cold and no long - er care for me.___
just a spark of the love___ that used to be.___

All my faith in you is gone___ but the heart - aches lin - ger on.___
If you love some - bod - y new,___ let me find___ a new love, too.___

Take These Chains from My Heart - 2 - 1

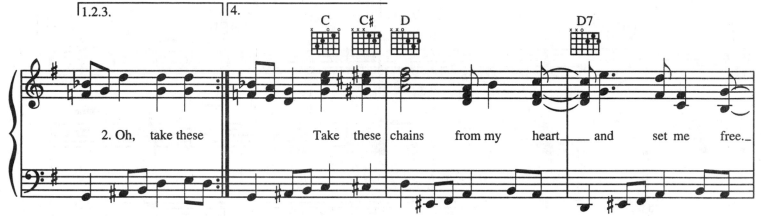

Repeat ad lib. and fade

Verse 3: Instrumental solo

Verse 4:
Give my heart just a word of sympathy.
Be as fair to my heart as you can be.
Then, if you no longer care for the love that's beating there,
Take these chains from my heart and set me free.

TENNESSEE WALTZ

Words and Music by
REDD STEWART and
PEE WEE KING

Moderately Slow

I was waltz-ing___ with my dar-lin'___ to the TEN - NES - SEE___

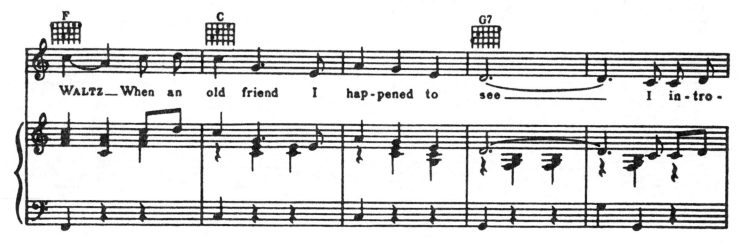

WALTZ___ When an old friend I hap-pened to see _____ I in-tro-

duced him___ to my loved one___ and___ while they___ were___ waltz-ing My

Tennessee Waltz - 2 - 1

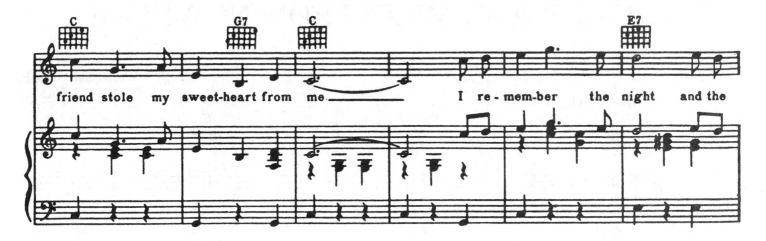

friend stole my sweet-heart from me._____ I re - mem - ber the night and the

TEN - NES - SEE Waltz Now I know just how much I have lost_____ Yes I

lost my___ lit - tle dar - lin'___ the___ night they___ were___ play - ing The

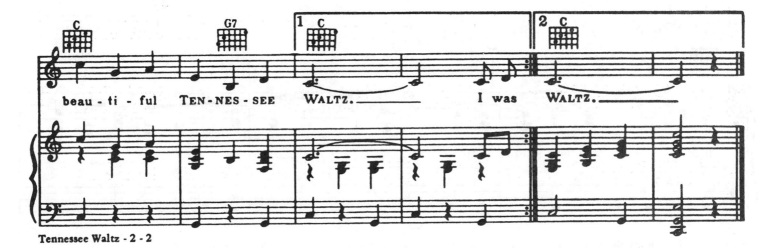

beau - ti - ful TEN - NES - SEE Waltz._____ I was Waltz._____

A THOUSAND MILES FROM NOWHERE

Words and Music by
DWIGHT YOAKAM

Moderately

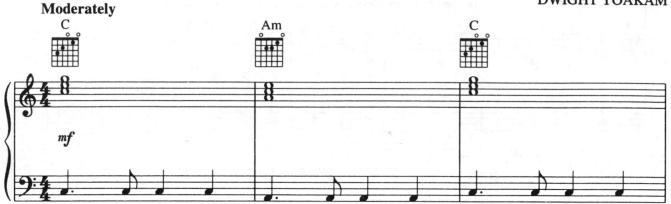

I'm a thou - sand miles __ from no - where,
time don't mat - ter to me. __ 'Cause I'm a thou - sand miles __ from no -

where and there's no __ place I __ want to be. __

A Thousand Miles from Nowhere - 4 - 1

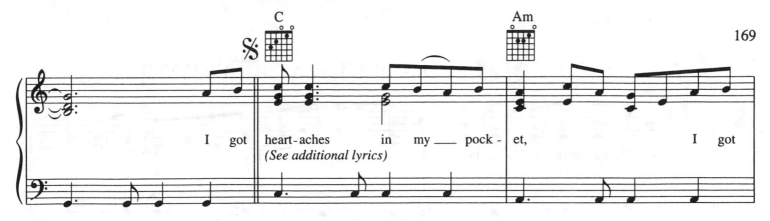

I got heart-aches in my ___ pock- et,   I got
(See additional lyrics)

ech - oes ___ in my ___ head ___   and all that I ___ keep __ hear-

ing   are the cruel, __ cruel things _ that you said. __

I'm a thou - sand miles ___ from no - where,

'Cause I'm a thou - sand miles ___ from no-

time don't mat- ter to me. __

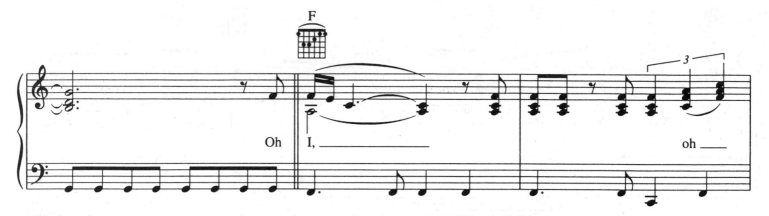

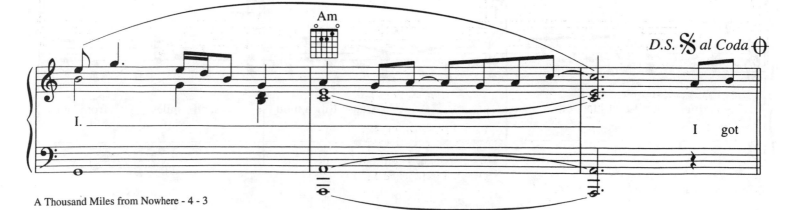

A Thousand Miles from Nowhere - 4 - 3

Repeat and fade (vocal ad lib)

Coda

I'm a thou - sand miles __ from no - where,

time don't mat - ter to me. ___ 'Cause I'm a thou -

sand miles ___ from no - where and there's no ___

__ place I ___ want to be. ___ I'm a thou -

A Thousand Miles from Nowhere - 4 - 4

Additional lyrics

2. I got bruises on my memory
I got tear stains on my hands
And in the mirror there's a vision
Of what used to be a man.

THEY'RE PLAYIN' OUR SONG

Words and Music by
BOB DIPIERO, JOHN JARRARD
and MARK D. SANDERS

Moderately ♩ = 88

Verse 1:

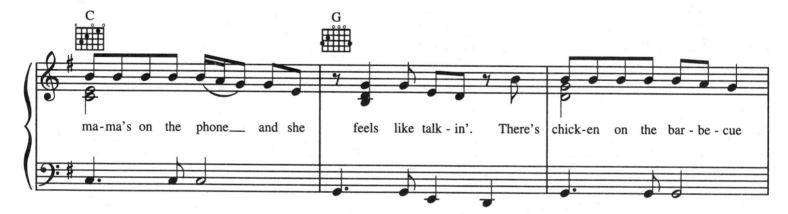

1. Some-bod-y's at the front door, I can hear 'em knock-in'. Your
2. *See additional lyrics*
3. *Instrumental*

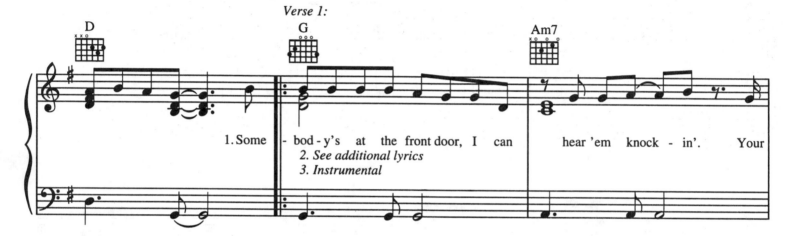

ma-ma's on the phone___ and she feels like talk-in'. There's chick-en on the bar-be-cue

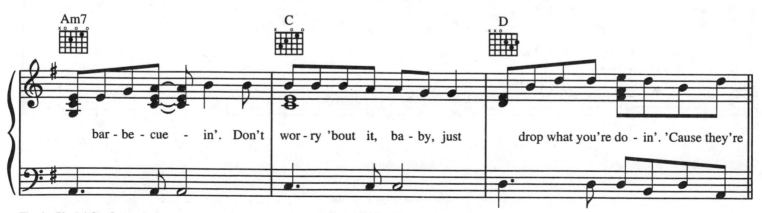

bar-be-cue-in'. Don't wor-ry 'bout it, ba-by, just drop what you're do-in'. 'Cause they're

They're Playin' Our Song - 4 - 1

Chorus:

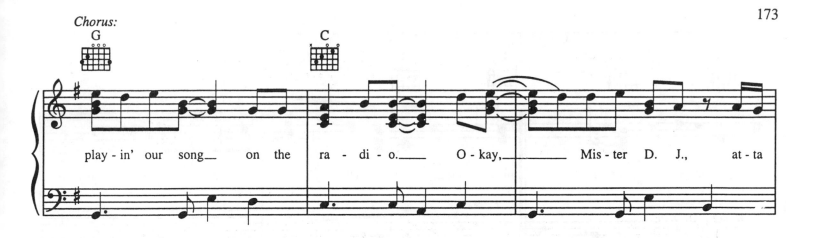

play - in' our song___ on the ra - di - o.___ O - kay,___ Mis - ter D. J., at - ta

way to go.___ A mil - lion watts of love___ pow - er com-in' on strong.___ Dance___

_____ with me dar - lin', they're play-in' our___ song.___

2. Oh the

2. D G **3.** D G

play-in' our___ song.___ play-in' our___ song.___ Oh, they're play - in' our song___ on the

C G D

ra - di - o.___ O - kay,___ Mis - ter D. J., at - ta way to go.___ A mil -

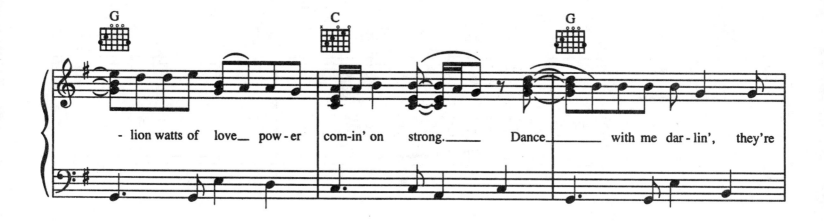

G C G

- lion watts of love___ pow-er com-in' on strong.___ Dance___ with me dar-lin', they're

D G C

play-in' our___ song.___

Repeat ad lib. and fade

Verse 2:
Oh, the house needs cleanin', the grass needs mowin',
We both got places that we need to be goin'.
Tomorrow's a big day, better get ready,
But tonight it's just you and me rockin' steady.
(To Chorus:)

THIS IS ME

Words and Music by
TOM SHAPIRO and TOM McHUGH

This Is Me - 4 - 1

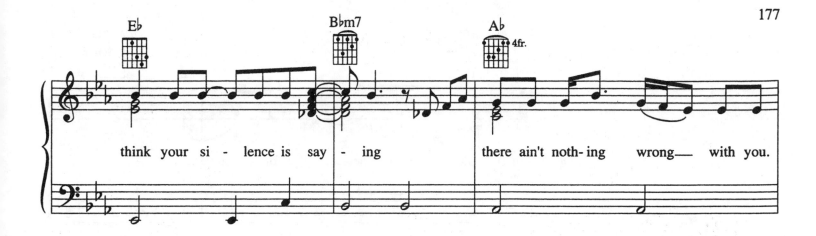

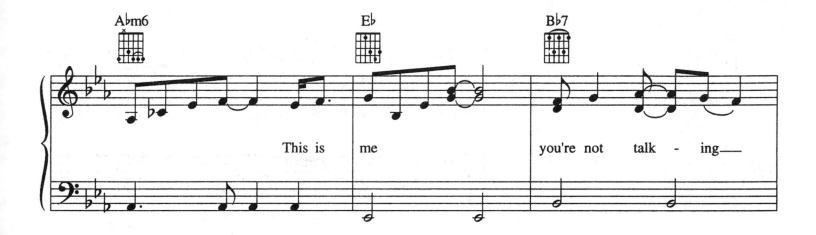

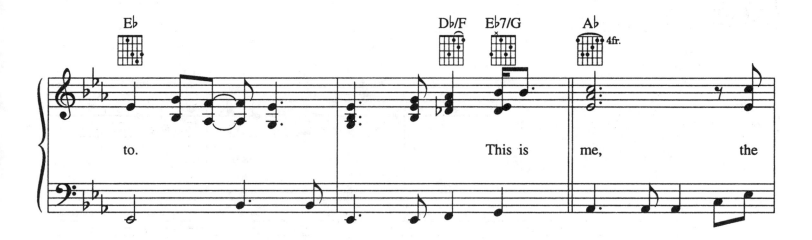

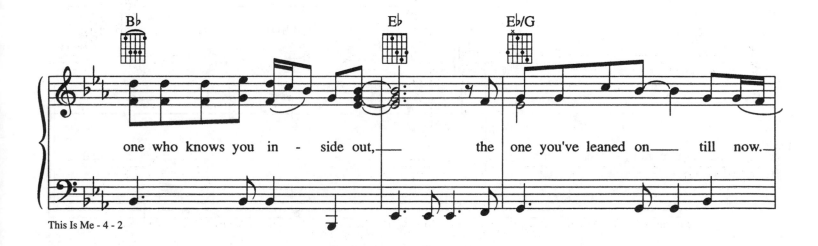

This Is Me - 4 - 2

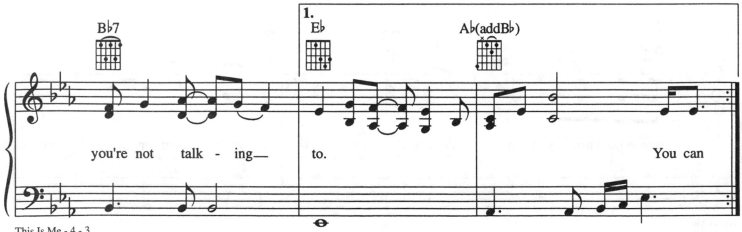

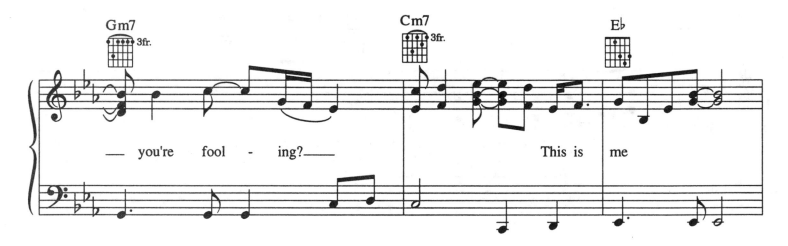

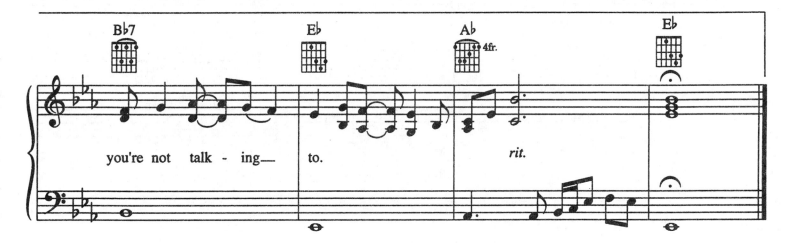

2.

Hey, this is me

you're not talk - ing— to. *rit.*

Additional lyrics

2. You can run to me no matter what you're running from.
   If it's something I'm doing, I'll get it undone,
   Just don't let me be a stranger to what you're going through,
   Hey, this is me you're not talking to.

(To Chorus)

YOUR LOVE AMAZES ME

Words and Music by
CHUCK JONES and AMANDA HUNT

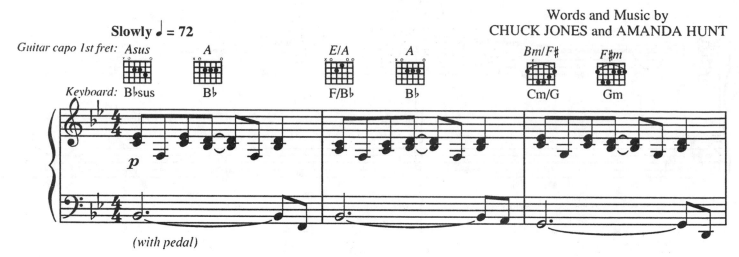

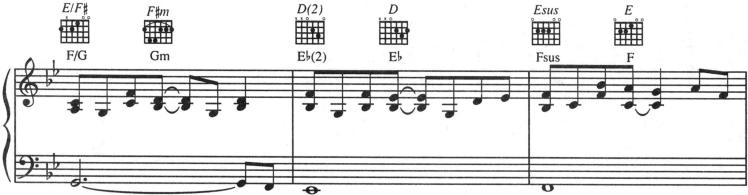

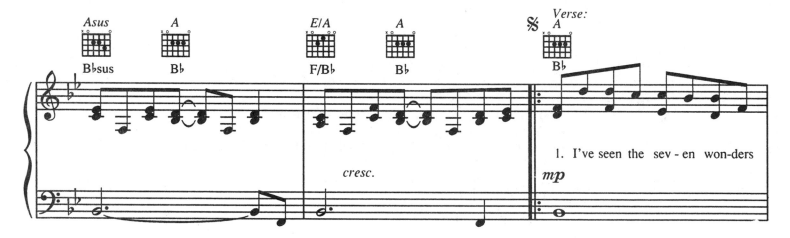

Your Love Amazes Me - 4 - 1

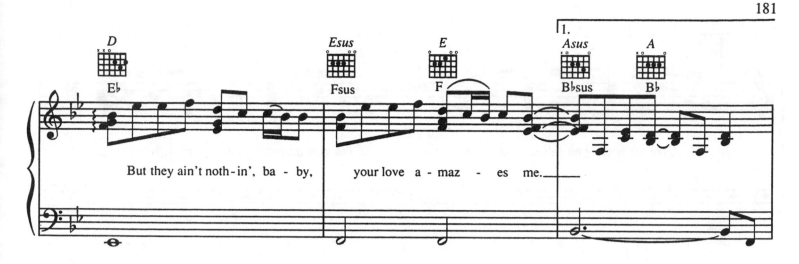

But they ain't noth-in', ba - by, your love a - maz - es me.

To next strain

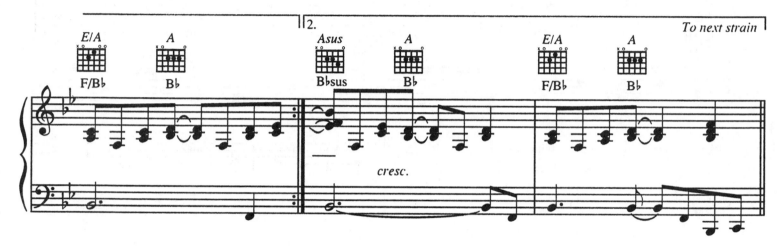

cresc.

cresc.

Chorus:

Don't you ev - er doubt this love of mine.

mf

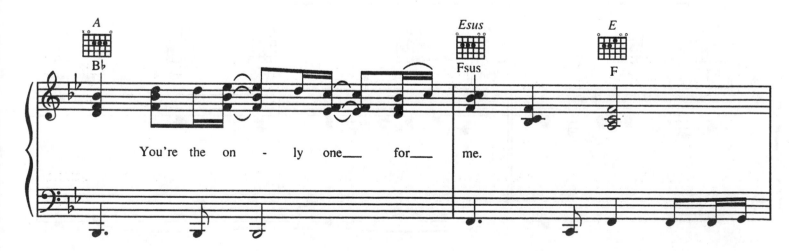

You're the on - ly one___ for___ me.

You give me hope, you give me rea-son. You give me some-thing to be-lieve in.

For-ev-er faith-ful-ly,___ you love a-maz-es me.___

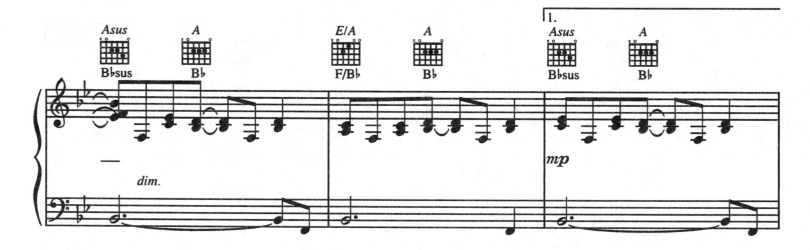

dim.

mp

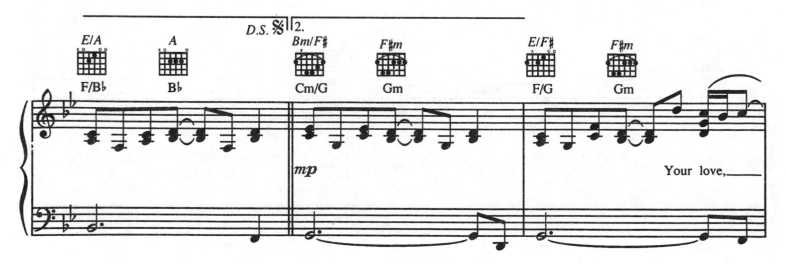

mp

Your love,___

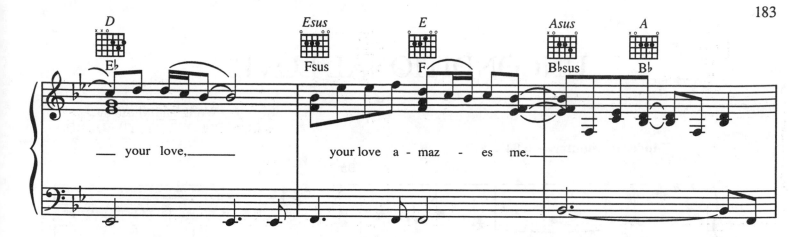

your love,_____ your love a - maz - es me._____

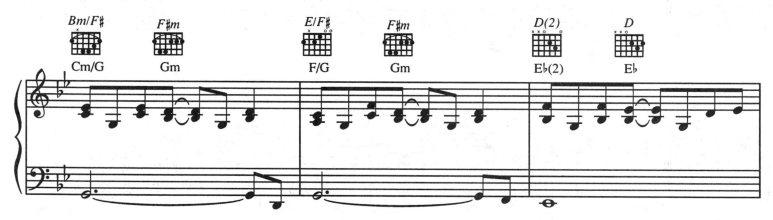

(Ad lib. vocals)

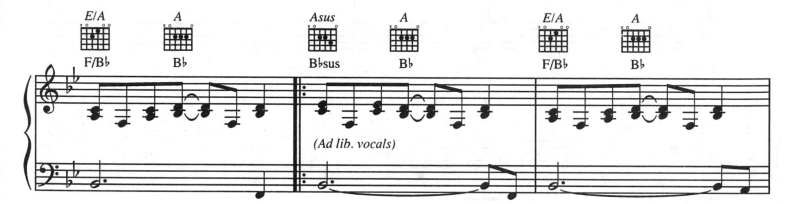

Repeat ad lib. and fade

Verse 2:
I've seen a sunset that would make you cry,
And colors of a rainbow reaching 'cross the sky.
The moon in all its phases, but
Your love amazes me.
To Chorus:

Verse 3:
I've prayed for miracles that never came.
I got down on my knees in the pouring rain.
But only you could save me,
Your love amazes me.
(To Chorus:)

UNCONDITIONAL LOVE

Words and Music by
DONNY LOWERY, TIM DUBOIS
and RANDY SHARP

Moderate country ♩ = 84

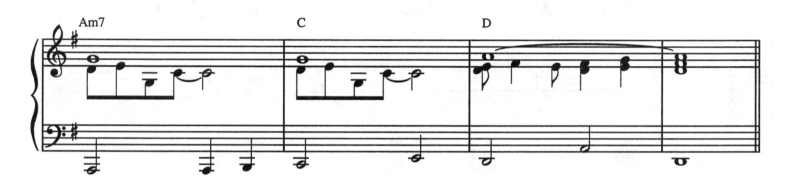

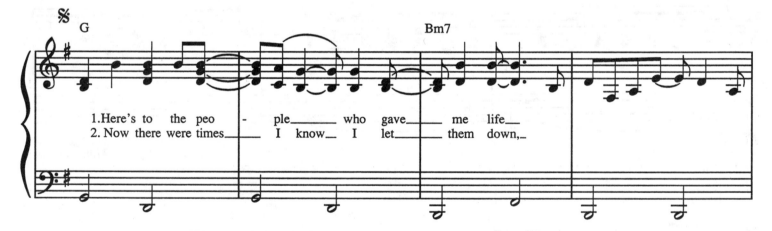

1. Here's to the peo - ple____ who gave____ me life____
2. Now there were times____ I know____ I let____ them down,____

and then showed me how to live____ it,____
but nev - er once was I re - ject - ed.____

Unconditional Love - 4 - 1

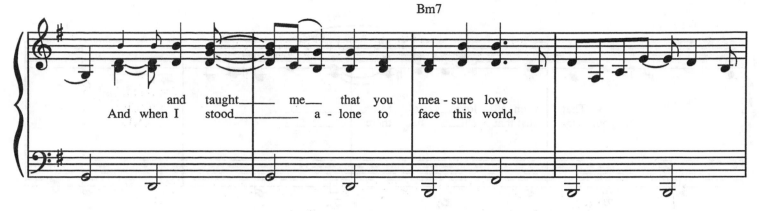

and taught___ me___ that you mea - sure love
And when I stood___ a - lone to face this world,

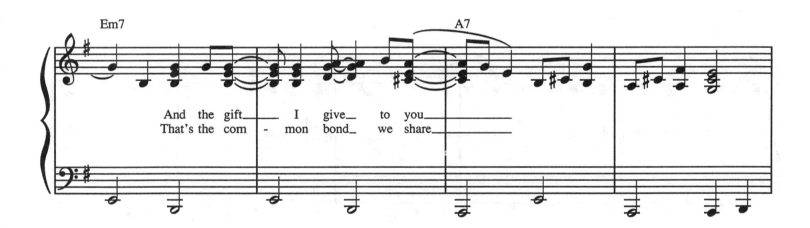

by how free - ly you can give___ it.___
some-how I___ still felt pro - tect - ed.___

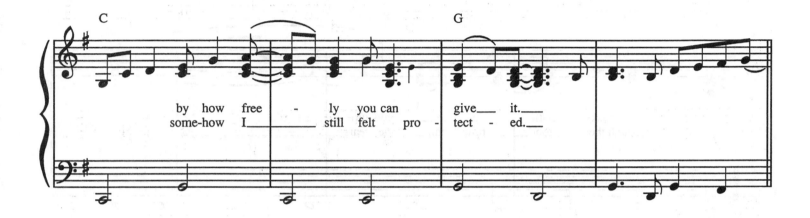

And the gift___ I give___ to you___
That's the com - mon bond___ we share___

is the les - son that___ I learned.___
and it will last___ through_ the years.___

That when a love___ is true,___
And you can trust that I'll___ be there___

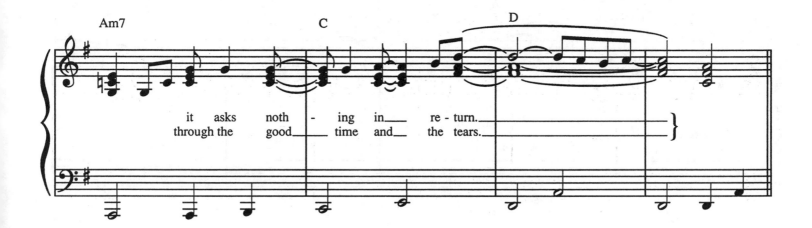

it asks noth - ing in___ re - turn.___
through the good___ time and___ the tears.___

Chorus:

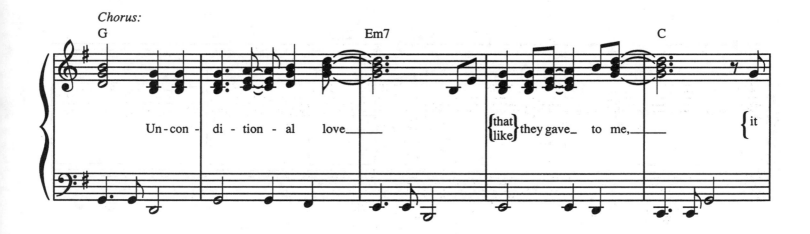

Un - con - di - tion - al love___ {that/like} they gave_ to me,___ {it

was - n't mine_}/it's not yours_} to keep,___ and_ I {knew/know} some - day___ {I'd hand it down_}/{some- one will look_} to you_

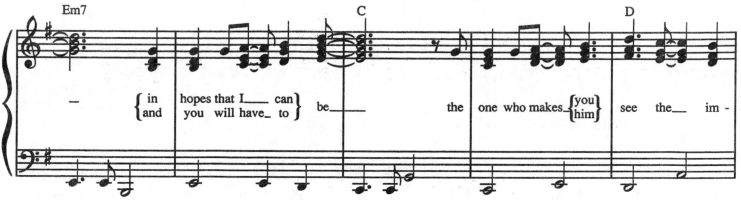

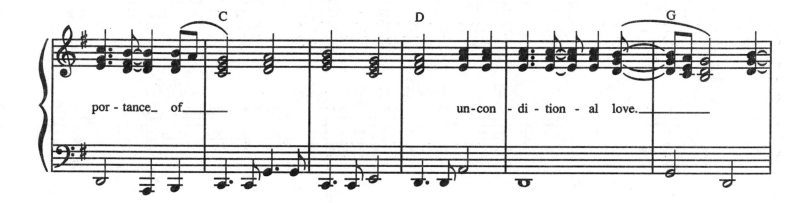

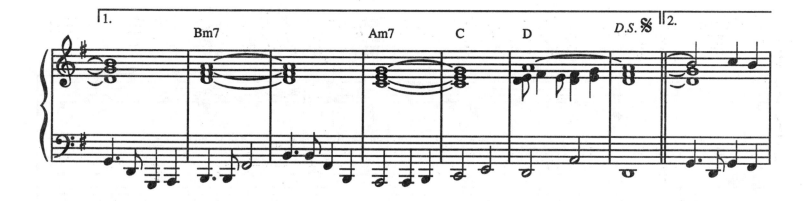

Unconditional Love - 4 - 4

UNTANGLIN' MY MIND

Words and Music by
CLINT BLACK and MERLE HAGGARD

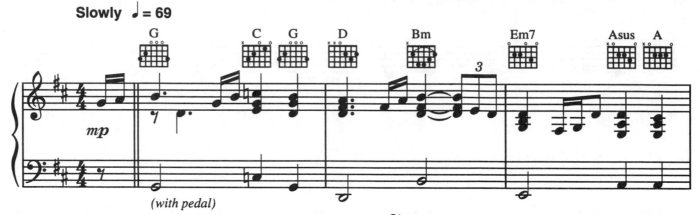

Untanglin' My Mind - 4 - 1

suit - case_____

and walk a - way from you___ the way I_____

___ should.   And   I can't seem to find___ the voice___ of rea-

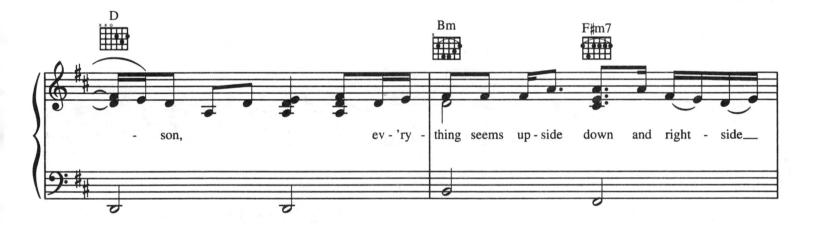

- son,   ev - 'ry - thing seems up - side down and right - side___

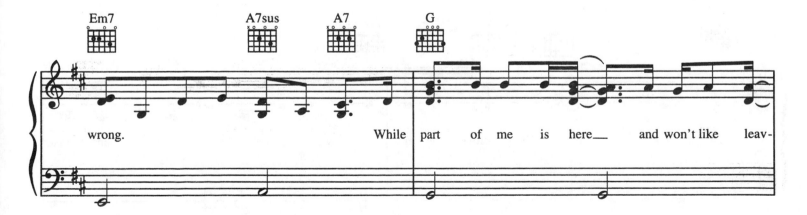

wrong.   While part of me is here___ and won't like leav-

- in',_____ the rest of me, the best of me___ is

gone.

cresc.

Chorus:

And I'm sure no one will won-der where I've gone___

mf

___ to,___ but if an-y-one should ask___ from time___ to time,

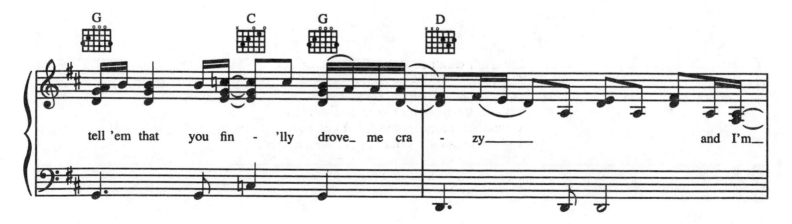

tell 'em that you fin-'lly drove___ me cra - zy_____ and I'm___

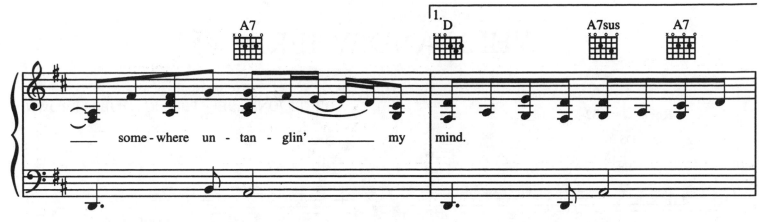

some-where un - tan - glin' my mind.

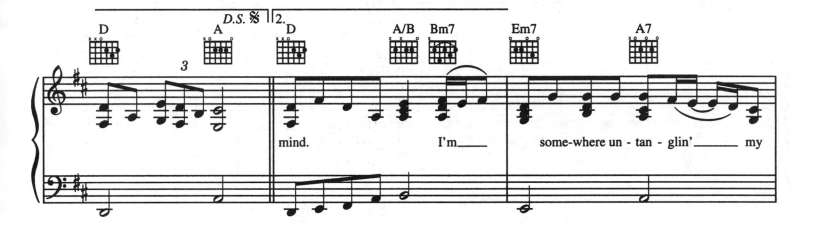

mind. I'm some-where un - tan - glin' my

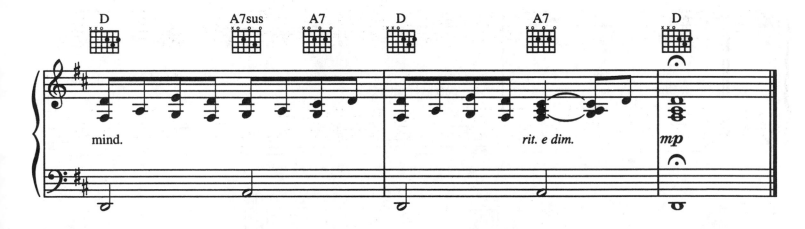

mind. *rit. e dim.* *mp*

Verse 2:
Tell 'em I won't be ridin', I'll be walkin'
'Cause I don't think a crazy man should drive.
Anyway, the car belongs to you, now,
Along with any part of me that's still alive.
But there's really not much left you could hold on to,
And if you did, it wouldn't last here, anyway.
It'd head to where the rest of me rolled on to,
So, even if I wanted to, I couldn't stay.
(To Chorus:)

WHEN AND WHERE

Words and Music by
BRETT JONES, JEFF PENNIG and JESS BROWN

When and Where - 4 - 1

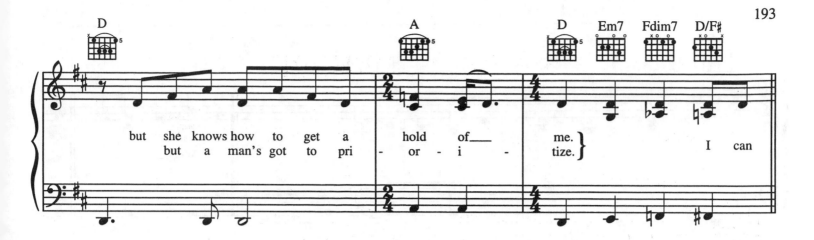

but she knows how to get a hold of___ me.}
but a man's got to pri - or - i - tize. I can

Chorus:

tell it's her by the way the phone rings. When she calls, I drop

ev-'ry-thing.___ Snaps her fin - gers___ and I'm there.___

"Hel-lo, dar-lin'. When_ and_ where?"_

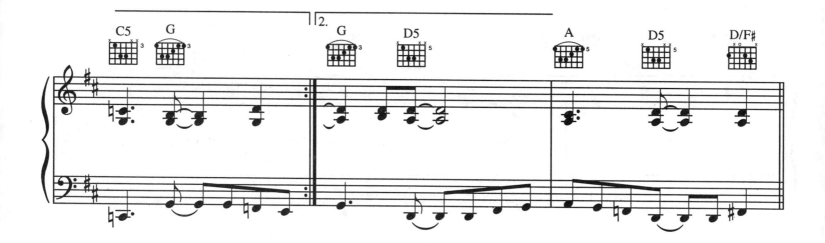

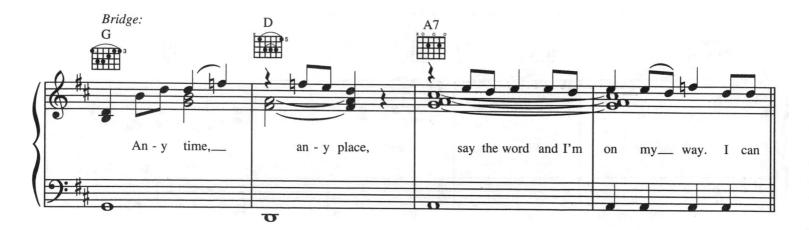

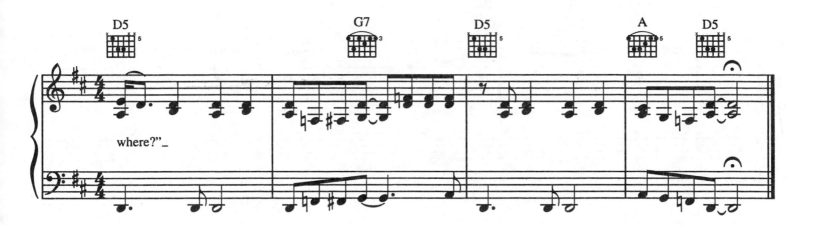

WHEN LOVE FINDS YOU

By VINCE GILL
and MICHAEL OMARTIAN

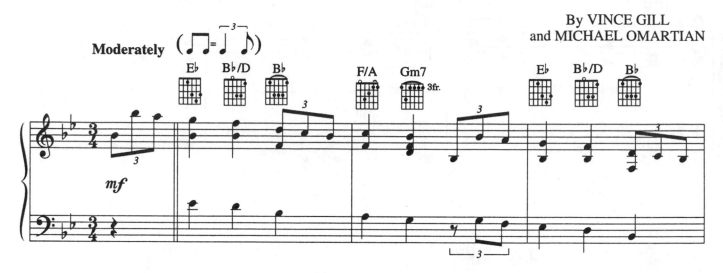

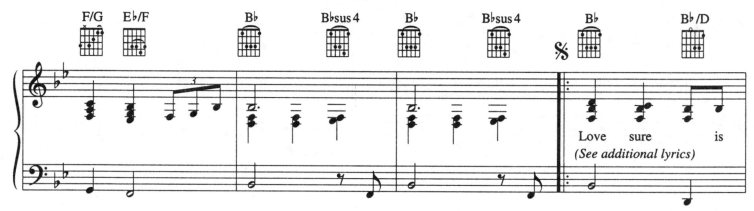

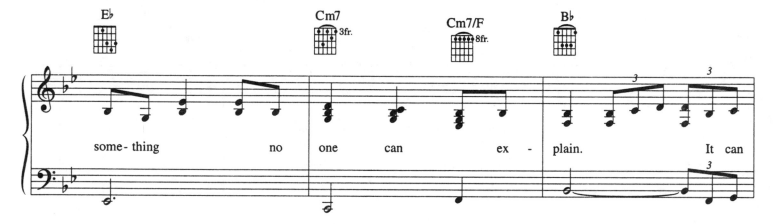

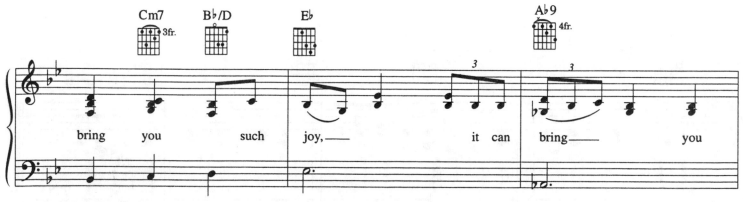

When Love Finds You - 4 - 1

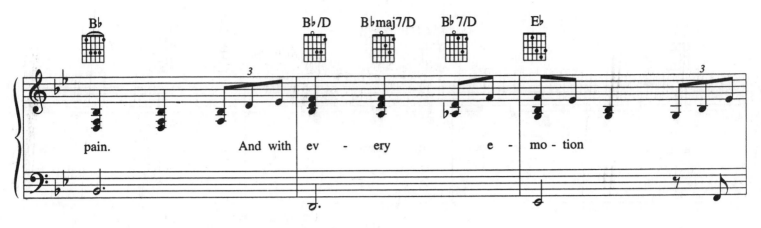

pain.   And with ev - ery   e - mo - tion

love puts us through,   there's noth - ing you can

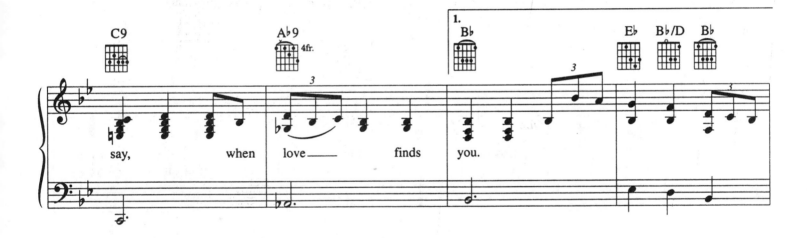

say,   when love___ finds you.

you.   Give it all you can

When Love Finds You - 4 - 2

198

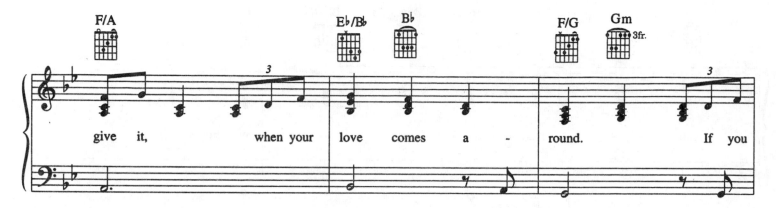

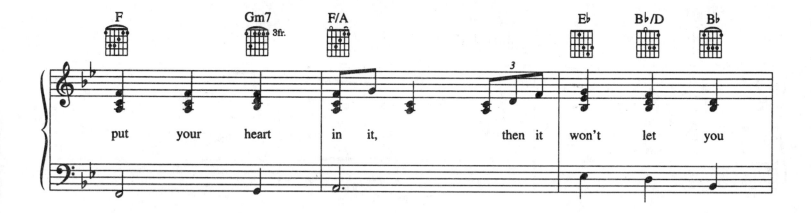

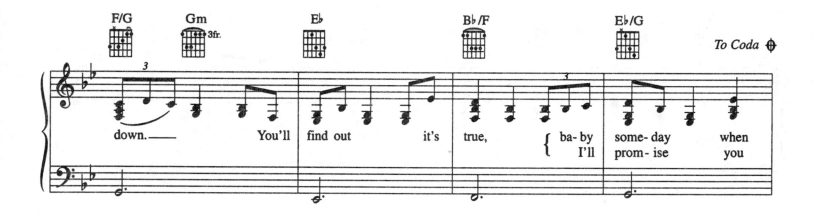

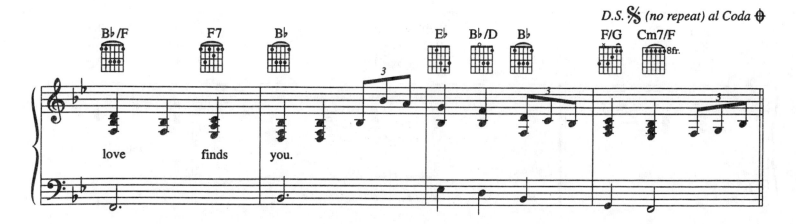

When Love Finds You - 4 - 3

199

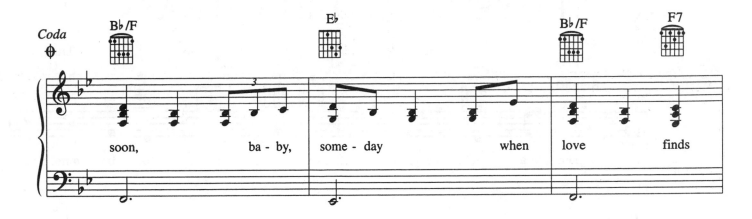

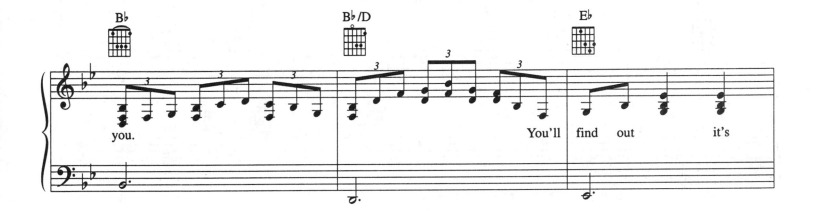

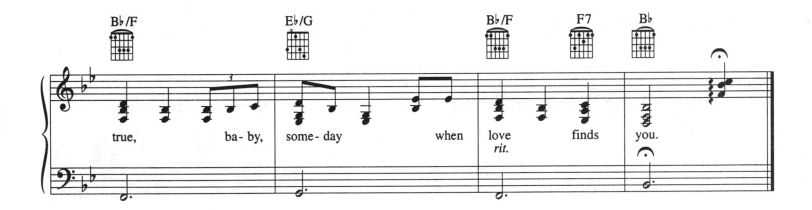

Additional lyrics

2. Love is the power that makes your heart beat,
   It can make you move mountains, make you drop to your knees.
   When it finally hits you, you won't know what to do,
   There's nothing you can say when love finds you.

3. *Instrumental*
   And when you least expect it, it will finally come true,
   There's nothing you can say when love finds you.

When Love Finds You - 4 - 4

THE YELLOW ROSE OF TEXAS

Traditional

The Yellow Rose Of Texas - 2 - 1

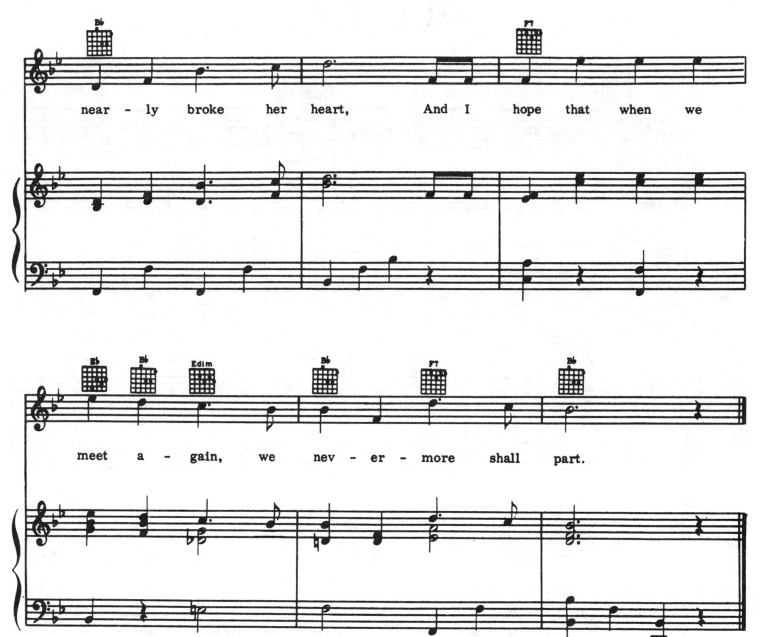

near - ly broke her heart, And I hope that when we

meet a - gain, we nev - er - more shall part.

2. She's the sweetest little lady a fellow ever knew,
   Her eyes are bright as diamonds, they sparkle like the dew.
   You may talk about your dearest girls, and sing of Rosalie,
   But the yellow rose of Texas beats the belles of Tennessee.

3. Down beside the Rio Grande, the stars were shining bright,
   We walked along together one quiet summer night,
   I hope that she remembers how we parted long ago,
   I'll keep my promise to return and never let her go.

4. There's a yellow rose in Texas, I'm going home to see.
   She wants no other fellow, nobody, only me.
   Oh, she cried so when I left her that it nearly broke her heart,
   And I hope that when we meet again, we never more shall part.

The Yellow Rose Of Texas - 2 - 2

YOU AND I

Moderately Slow and Smooth

Words and Music by
FRANK MYERS

You And I - 4 - 1

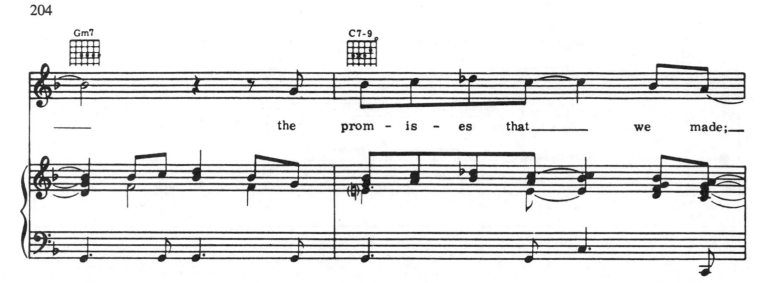

the prom - is - es that _____ we made; _____

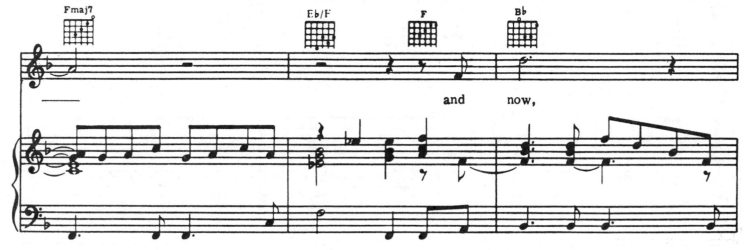

and now,

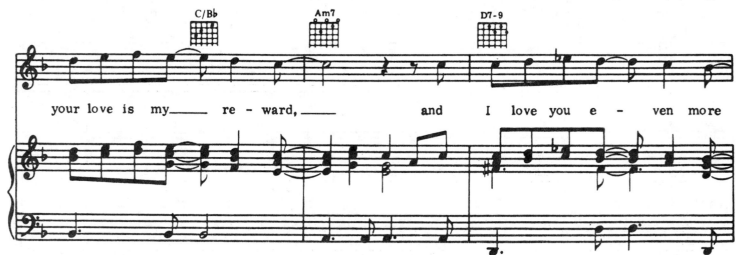

your love is my _____ re - ward, _____ and I love you e - ven more

than I .ev - er did _____ be - fore. _____

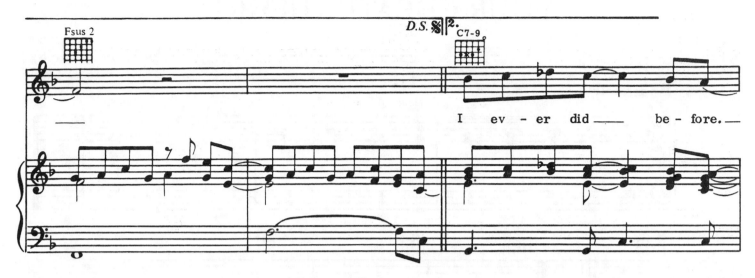

Verse 3:
Just you and I;
We care and trust each other.
With you in my life,
There'll never be another.
We'll be all right,
Just you and I.
(To Chorus:)

YOUR CHEATIN' HEART

Words and Music by
HANK WILLIAMS

Your Cheatin' Heart - 2 - 1

BABY LIKES TO ROCK IT

Words and Music by
STEVE RIPLEY and W. RICHMOND

Lyrics: Ba-by likes to rock it like a boog-ie woog-ie choo-choo train, _____ train.

Lyrics: Train, train, train, _____ train. _____

(drums)

Baby Likes to Rock It - 5 - 1

Verse 2:
Johnny's in the back room suckin' on his gin,
Police are at the front door, screamin, "Let me in!"
Go-go-go-go dancer busy showin' off her chest,
She don't know what she doin' but she tries her best.
(To Bridge & Chorus:)

Verse 3:
She said her name was "Emergency" and asked to see my gun,
Said her telephone number was 9-1-1.
Got Brother Jimmy on the TV, Keillor on a stereo,
Said, "If you wanna get it, you got to let it go."
(To Bridge & Chorus:)

A BAD GOODBYE

Words and Music by
CLINT BLACK

sure   those eyes   won't____   cry._____   And in my   mind   I've_ left   e -

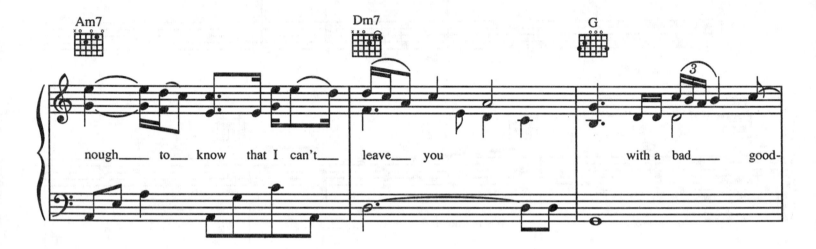

nough____ to_ know   that I can't___   leave___ you   with a bad____   good-

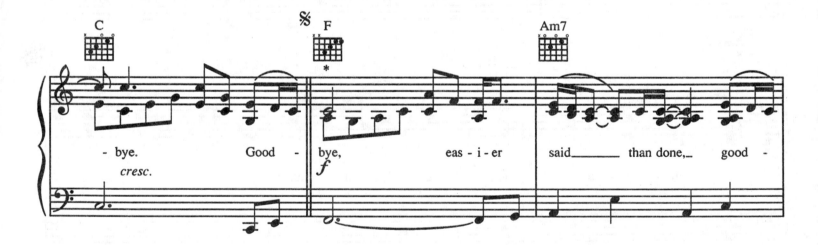

- bye.   Good - bye,   eas - i - er   said_____ than done,__   good -
cresc.   ƒ

bye.___   There's no good_ when   you're___ the one_ whose good - bye_____ you swore_
        (On D.S., rit.)   (On D.S., a tempo)

*Sung 8va on D.S.

To Coda ⊕

would nev-er____come and____ in my_____ good-bye,_ you're find - ing none.

dim.

I'm still bound to leave_ you, I sure-ly don't know__

mf

__ how. My heart won't let me put__ you through_ what my mind__

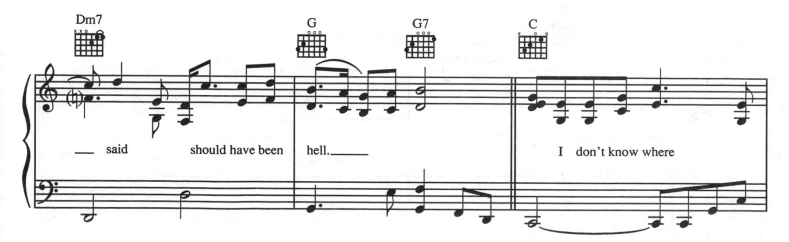

__ said should have been hell.____ I don't know where

we'll go____ from here,_____ there may be____ ___ no way to_____

fly._____ And the cloud I'm in just__ makes it all__

_____ too__ clear that I can't____ leave____ you with__ a

bad_____ good - bye._____ Good -

D.S. 𝄋 al Coda

Sung 8va

cresc.

⊕ *Coda*

How can we be so far__ be - tween_____ where we

are and one more___ try?_____ And an-y way I__ look, I've on-

-ly__seen that I can't__ leave__ you with_ a bad_____ good -

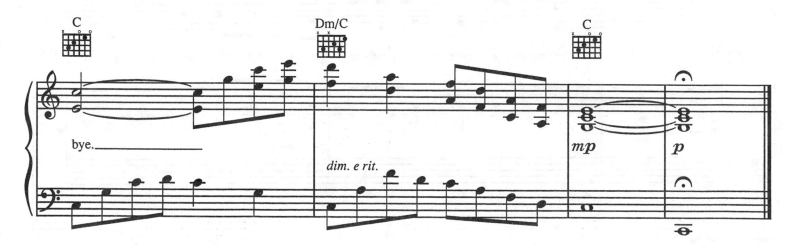

bye._____ *dim. e rit.*

BEHIND CLOSED DOORS

Words and Music by
KENNY O'DELL

Moderate

ba - by makes me proud, Lord, don't she make —— me proud.

She nev - er makes a scene by hang - in' all o - ver me in a

Behind Closed Doors - 3 - 1

crowd,_____ 'Cause peo - ple like to talk, _____

Lord, don't they love _____ to talk. But when they

turn out the ___ lights, I know she'll be leav - in' ___ with me;

And when we get be - hind closed ___ doors, then she lets her

hair hang down, and she makes me glad I'm a man; Oh, no one knows what goes on be - hind closed doors.

1. My
2. be - hind closed doors.

2. My baby makes me smile, Lord, don't she make me smile.
She's never far away or too tired to say I want you.
She's always a lady, just like a lady should be
But when they turn out the lights, she's still a baby to me.

BLUE MOON OF KENTUCKY

Words and Music by
BILL MONROE

Blue moon, _____ blue moon, _____ blue moon _____ keep a-shin-in' bright. _____ Blue moon keep—on a-shin-in' bright,_ you're gon-na bring-a me back - a my ba-by to-night; blue moon

Blue Moon Of Kentucky - 3 - 1

Chorus:

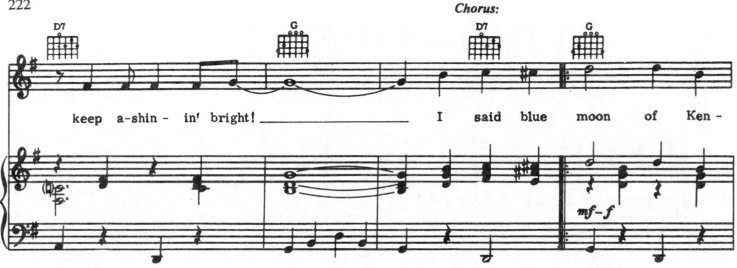

keep a-shin-in' bright! _____ I said blue moon of Ken-

tuck-y, to keep on shin-ing, _____ shine on the one that's gone and left me blue. _____

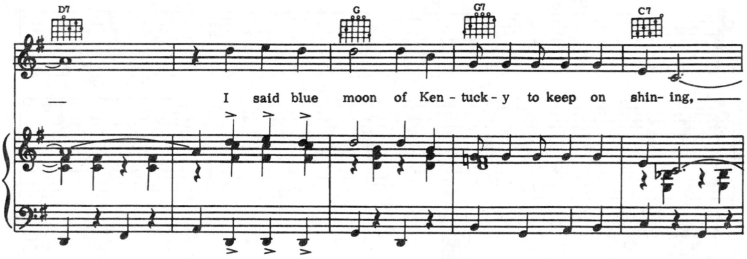

_____ I said blue moon of Ken-tuck-y to keep on shin-ing, _____

_____ shine on the one that's gone and left _____ me blue. _____

Blue Moon Of Kentucky - 3 - 2

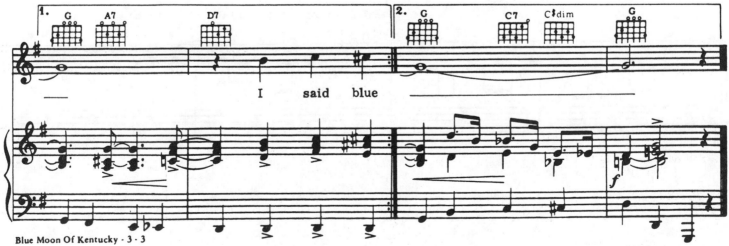

Blue Moon Of Kentucky - 3 - 3

CITY OF NEW ORLEANS

Words and Music by
STEVE GOODMAN

City Of New Orleans - 5 - 2

I'll be gone____ five hun - dred miles ____ when the day ____ is

done.

2. Dealin' card games with the old men in the club car,
Penny a point ain't no one keepin' score.
Pass the paper bag that holds the bottle;
Feel the wheels grumblin' 'neath the floor;
And the sons of Pullman porters, and the sons of engineers
Ride their father's magic carpet made of steel.
Mothers with their babes asleep are rockin' to the gentle beat
And the rhythm of the rails is all they feel.

3. Night time on the City of New Orleans,
Changin' cars in Memphis, Tennessee;
Halfway home, we'll be there by mornin',
Thru the Mississippi darkness rollin' down to the sea.
But all the towns and people seem to fade into a bad dream,
And the steel rail still ain't heard the news;
The conductor sings his songs again;
The passengers will please refrain,
This train's got the disappearin' railroad blues.

DEJA BLUE

Moderately ♩ = 104

Words and Music by
CRAIG WISEMAN and DONNIE LOWERY

Verses 1 & 2:

1. Now, as she's walk-ing out the door,____
2. *See additional lyrics*

say-in' she don't want me no more,____ as her ti - res are a-squeal-in', Lord, I

get this fun-ny feel-in' that I've been in this po-si-tion be-fore.__

Deja Blue - 5 - 1

Tell me will it nev-er end. Same ol'

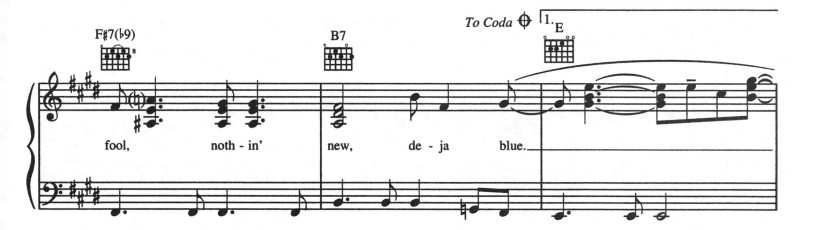

fool, noth-in' new, de-ja blue.

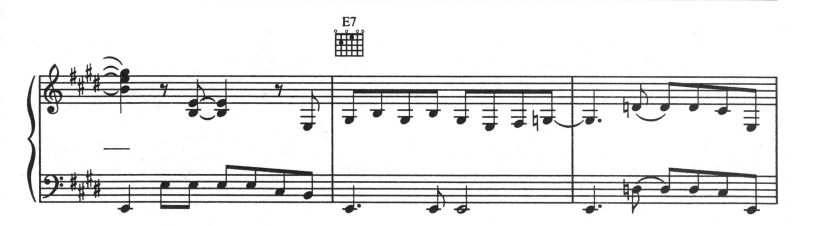

2. Now it

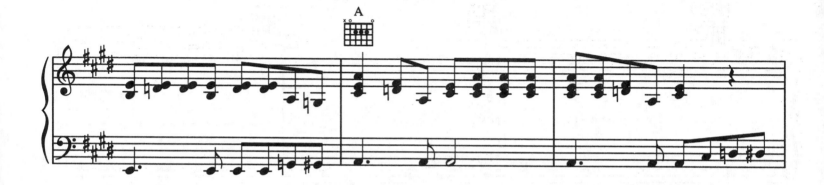

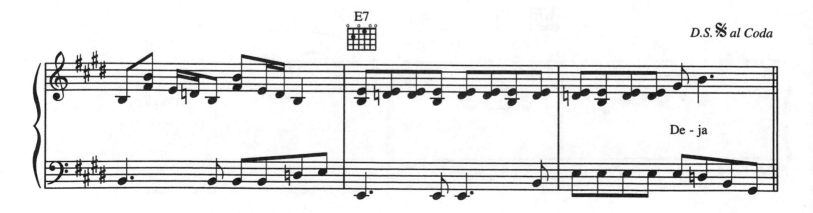

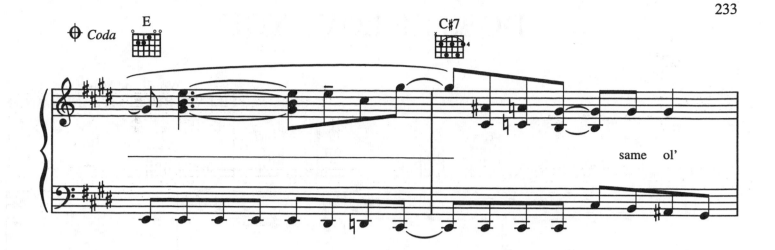

Verse 2:
Now, it started in the second grade,
With little blondie what's her name.
Yeah, I toted all her books
And gave her long and gooshy looks,
But all she wanted was my brother Ray.
That first time nearly done me in,
But I've been there a hundred times since then.
(To Chorus:)

Deja Blue - 5 - 5

DOES HE LOVE YOU

Words and Music by
BILLY STRITCH and SANDY KNOX

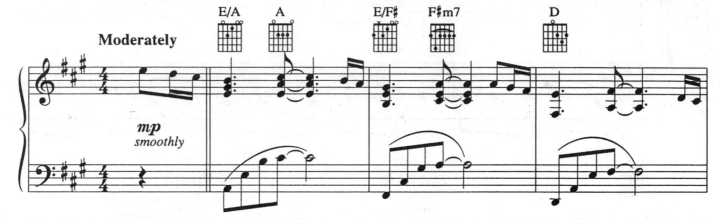

I've known a-bout you _____ for a while now. _____ When he

leaves me _____ he wears a smile _____ now _____ as soon as he's _____ a-way from

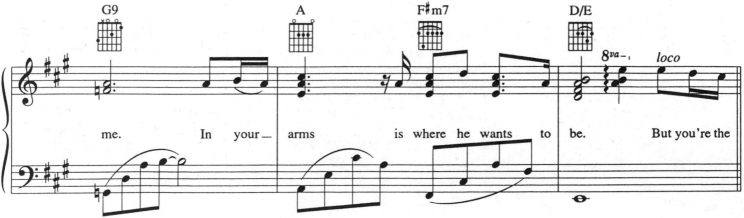

me. In your _____ arms is where he wants to be. But you're the

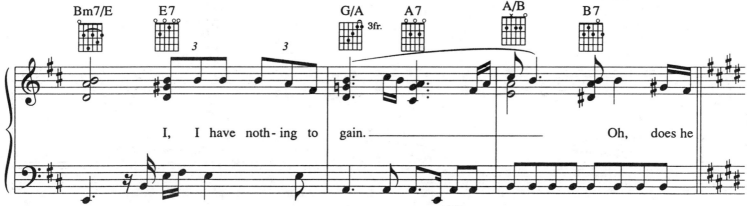

Additional Lyrics

2. But when he's with me, he says he needs me
   And that he wants me, that he believes in me.
   And when I'm in his arms, oh, he swears there's no one else.
   Is he deceiving me or am I deceiving myself?
   (To Chorus)

DON'T ROCK THE JUKEBOX

Words and Music by
ALAN JACKSON, KEITH STEGALL
and ROGER MURRAH

Moderate country shuffle ♩ = 144

Don't Rock the Jukebox - 3 - 1

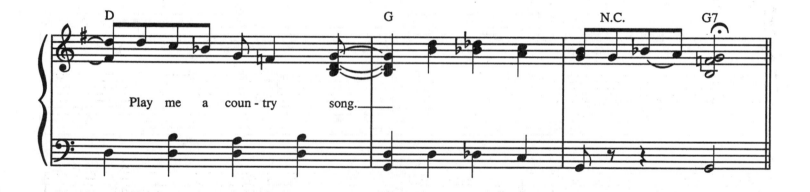

Verse 2:
I ain't got nothin' against rock and roll.
But when your heart's been broken, you need a song that's slow.
Ain't nothin' like a steel guitar to drown a memory.
Before you spend your money, babe, play a song for me.
(To Chorus:)

EAGLE WHEN SHE FLIES

Moderate country waltz ♩ = 88

Words and Music by
DOLLY PARTON

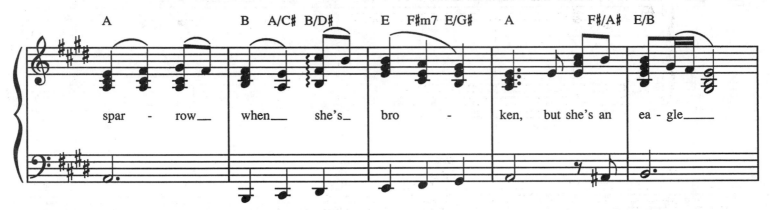

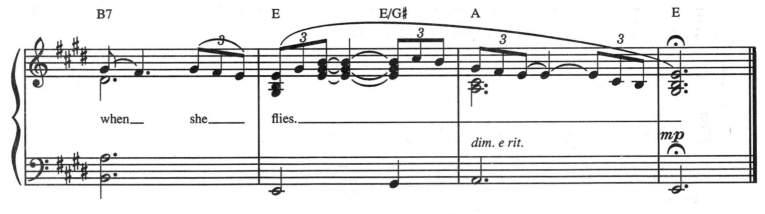

Verse 2:
A kaleidoscope of colors you can toss
Her around and 'round.
You can keep her in your vision,
But you'll never keep her down.
She's a lover, she's a mother,
She's a friend, and she's a wife.
And she's a sparrow when she's broken,
But she's an eagle when she flies.
(To Chorus:)

EASY COME, EASY GO

Words and Music by
DEAN DILLON and AARON BARKER

Moderate country rock ♩ = 100

1. Says she's had e-nough of me. I've had e-nough of her too. Might as well go on and set her free.___ She's al-read-y turned me___ loose. No fault, no blame, no-bod-y

Easy Come, Easy Go - 3 - 1

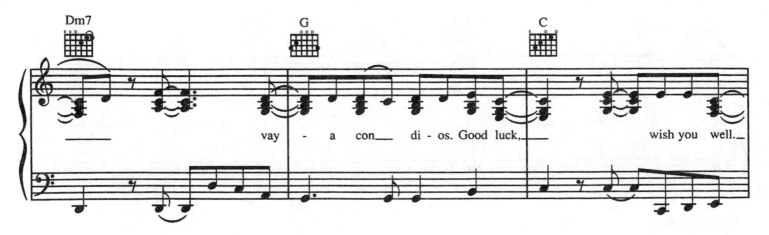

Take it slow; _____ eas - y come, _____ girl, _____ eas - y

go.

1. | D.S. %‖ 2. 3. etc. | Repeat ad lib. and fade

Verse 2:
Tried to work it out a hundred times;
Ninety-nine, it didn't work.
I think it's best to put it all behind
Before we wind up getting hurt.
No hard feelings, darling, no regrets,
No tears and no broken hearts.
Call it quits, callin' off all bets.
It just wasn't in the cards.
(To Chorus:)

Easy Come, Easy Go - 3 - 3

ELVIRA

Words and Music by
DALLAS FRAZIER

Elvira - 3 - 1

girl can sho' nuff make my lit-tle light shine _____

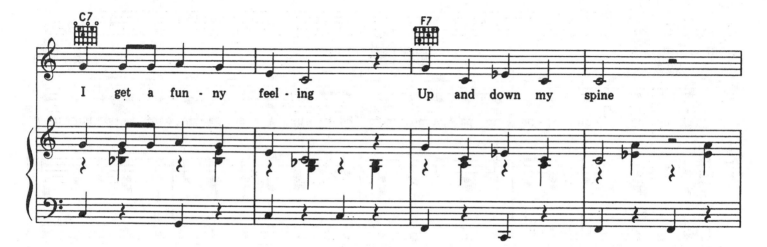

I get a fun-ny feel-ing Up and down my spine

'Cause I know that my EL - VIR - A's mine _____

CHORUS I

I'm sing-in' EL - VIR - A, EL - VIR - A, My

Elvira - 3 - 2

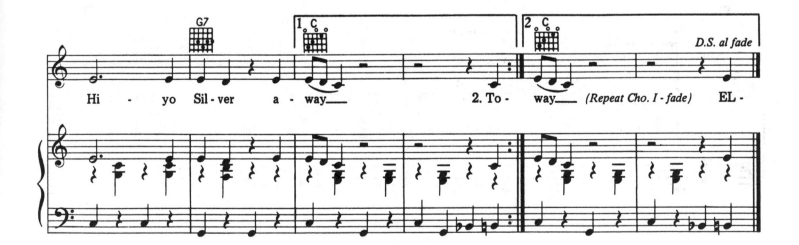

Verse 2
Tonight I'm gonna meet her
At the hungry house cafe
And I'm gonna give her all the love I can
She's gonna jump and holler
'Cause I saved up my last two dollar
And we're gonna search and find that preacher man

Chorus

FOREVER'S AS FAR AS I'LL GO

Words and Music by
MIKE REID

Forever's As Far As I'll Go - 3 - 1

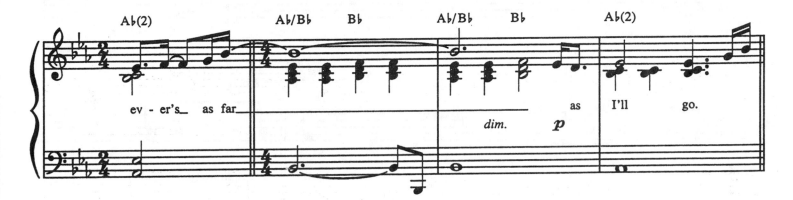

Verse 2:
When there's age around my eyes and gray in your hair,
And it only takes a touch to recall the love we've shared.
I won't take for granted that you know my love is true.
Each night in your arms, I will whisper to you...
(To Chorus:)

Forever's As Far As I'll Go - 3 - 3

IF I COULD MAKE A LIVING

Moderate country two-beat ♩ = 72

Words and Music by
ALAN JACKSON, KEITH STEGALL
and ROGER MURRAH

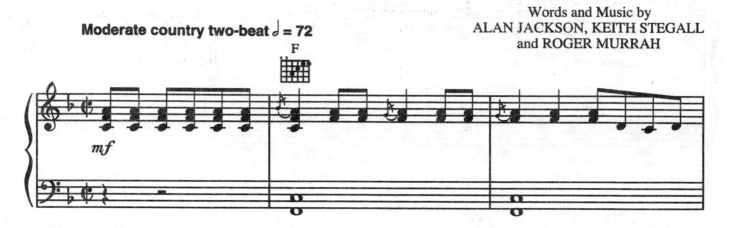

Chorus:

If I could make a liv-ing out of

lov-ing you,___ I'd be a mil-lion-aire in a week or two.___ I'd be

do-ing what I love and lov-ing what I do___ if I could make a liv-ing out of

If I Could Make a Living - 5 - 1

lov - ing___ you.

1. Ear - ly ev - 'ry morn-ing when the
2. *See additional lyrics.*

sun comes up___ I'm punch-in' that clock_ on the wall; break-in' my back just to

make a buck,_ wish-ing I was in your arms._____ If

Chorus:

I could make a liv-ing out of lov - ing you,___ I'd be a mil-lion-aire in a

week or two.___ I'd be do-ing what I love and lov - ing what I do___ if

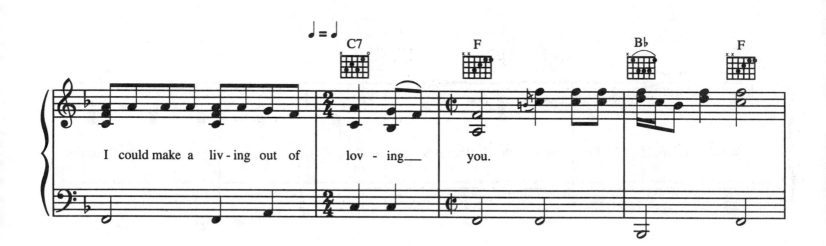

I could make a liv-ing out of lov-ing___ you.

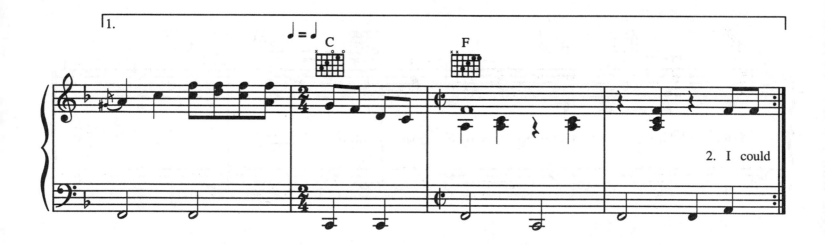

2. I could

Chorus:

If I could make a liv-ing out of lov-ing you,___ I'd

be a mil-lion-aire in a week or two.___ I'd be do-ing what I love and lov-

-ing what I do___ if I could make a liv-ing out of lov-ing___ you. If

Chorus:

I could make a liv-ing out of lov-ing you,___ I'd be a mil-lion-aire in a

If I Could Make a Living - 5 - 4

week or two.___ I'd be do-ing what I love and lov - ing what I do___ if

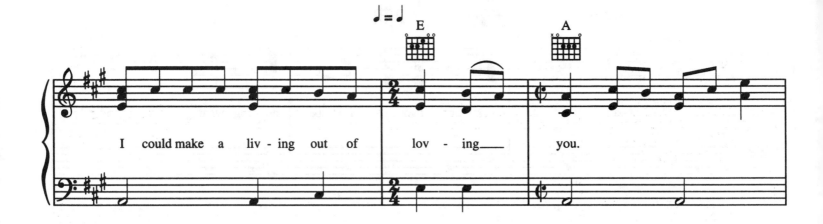

I could make a liv - ing out of lov - ing___ you.

Verse 2:
I could work all day and feel right at home
Loving that 8 to 5,
And never have to leave you here alone
When I'm working over-time.
(To Chorus:)

If I Could Make a Living - 5 - 5

IN THIS LIFE

Words and Music by
MIKE REID and
ALLEN SHAMBLIN

In This Life - 3 - 1

With one hon - est touch you set me free.___ Let the

Chorus:

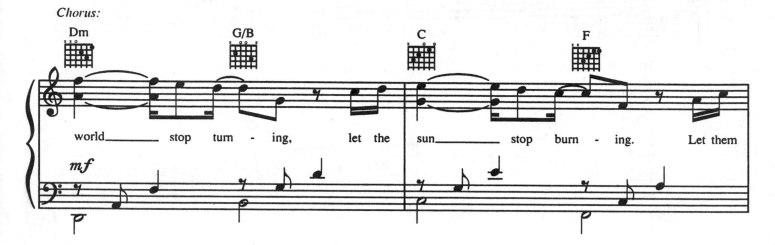

world___ stop turn - ing, let the sun___ stop burn - ing. Let them

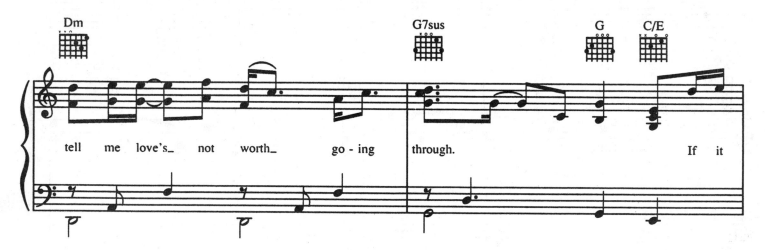

tell me love's_ not worth_ go - ing through. If it

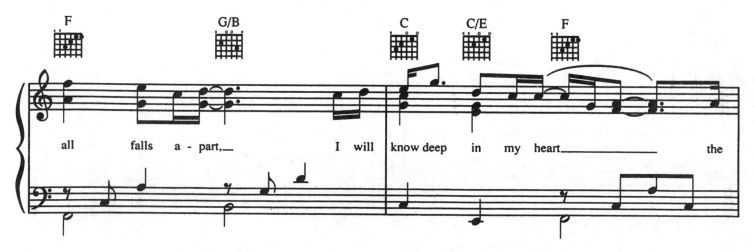

all falls a - part,___ I will know deep in my heart___ the

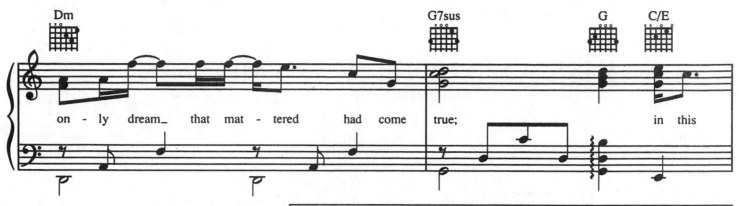

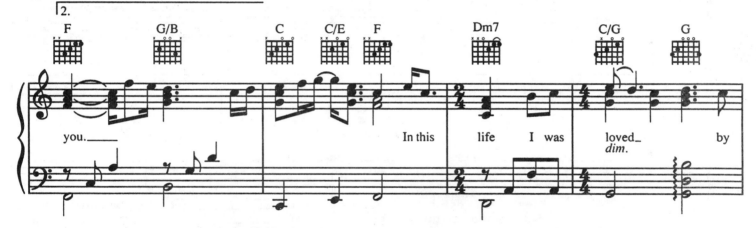

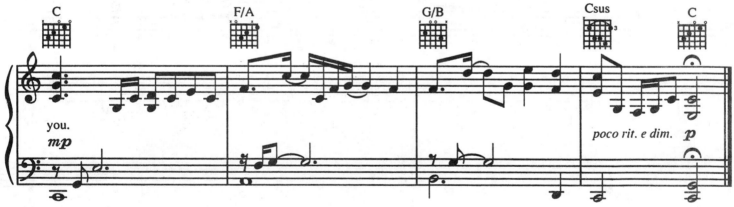

Verse 2:
For every mountain I have climbed.
Every raging river crossed,
You were the treasure that I longed to find.
Without your love I would be lost.
(To Chorus:)

KISS AN ANGEL GOOD MORNIN'

Words and Music by
BEN PETERS

Kiss An Angel Good Mornin' - 3 - 1

Kiss An Angel Good Mornin' - 3 - 2

Kiss An An - gel Good Morn - in' and love her like the dev - il when you get back home.

2. Well, get back home.

get back home.

Kissin' An Angel Good Mornin' - 3 - 3

LOOK WHAT FOLLOWED ME HOME

Words and Music by
TOMMY POLK and DAVID BALL

Look What Followed Me Home - 3 - 1

on a mid-night ride down a dark and lone-ly back road and

left it there to die. Look what fol-lowed me home!

Chorus:

I thought I was a-lone but your mem-o-ry is com-ing back to me.

I thought I'd left it be-hind

and had you off my mind._____ But I see I was wrong,—

___ wrong,— wrong.— Look what fol-lowed me home!_____ 2. Well, I

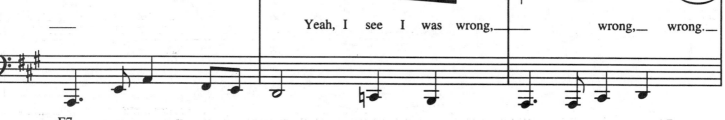

___ Yeah, I see I was wrong,—— wrong,— wrong.

___ Look what fol-lowed me home!___

Verse 2:
Well, I walked down to the river at the break of dawn
With a picture of you, darling, up underneath my arm.
I said, "The heartache's over, today is your last day."
And I thanked that muddy river as it carried you away.
(To Chorus:)

LOST IN THE FIFTIES TONIGHT
(In the Still of the Night)

Words and Music by
MIKE REID, TROY SEALS
and FRED PARRIS

50's Rock feel

Close your eyes__ ba - by, fol - low my heart;__ call on the mem - 'ries__
These prec - ious__ hours__ we know can't sur - vive,____ but love's all that mat - ters__

here in the dark.____ We'll let the mag - ic__ take__ us a - way,__
while the past is a - live.____ Now and for al - ways,__ time__ dis - ap - pears,__

Lost in the Fifties Tonight - 3 - 1

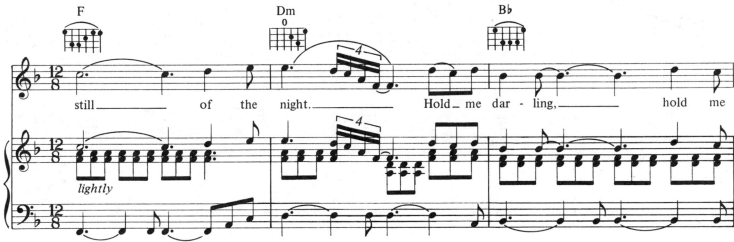

Lost in the Fifties Tonight - 3 - 2

MI VIDA LOCA
(MY CRAZY LIFE)

Words and Music by
PAM TILLIS and JESS LEARY

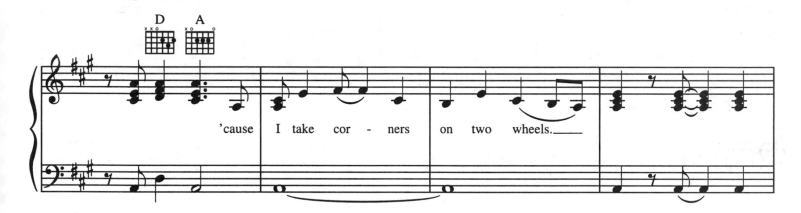

Mi Vida Loca - 5 - 1

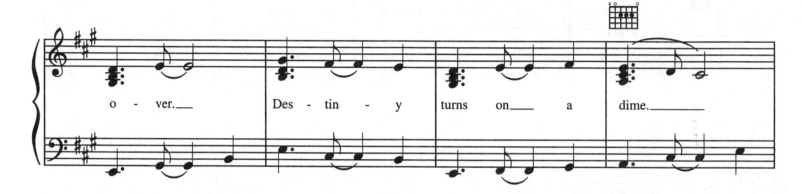

2. Sweet - life.

Bridge:

Here in____ the fire - light___ I see your___ tat - oo.

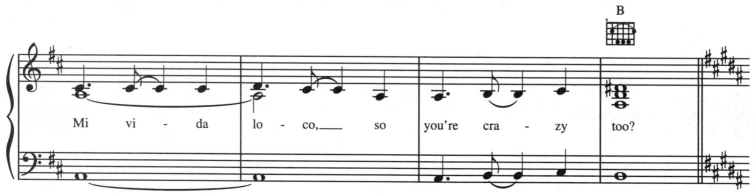

Mi vi - da lo - co,___ so you're cra - zy too?

Chorus:

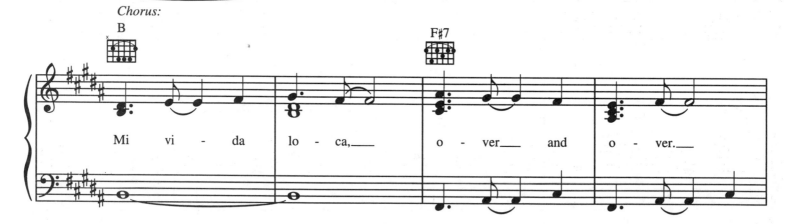

Mi vi - da lo - ca,___ o - ver___ and o - ver.___

Des - tin - y turns on___ a dime.___ We'll

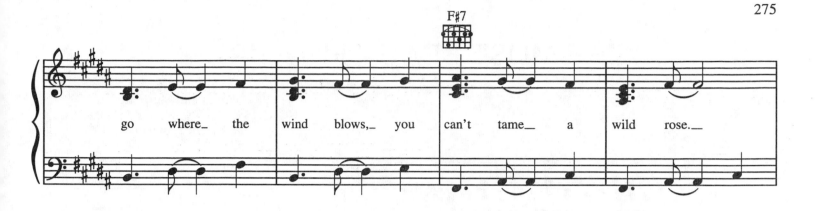

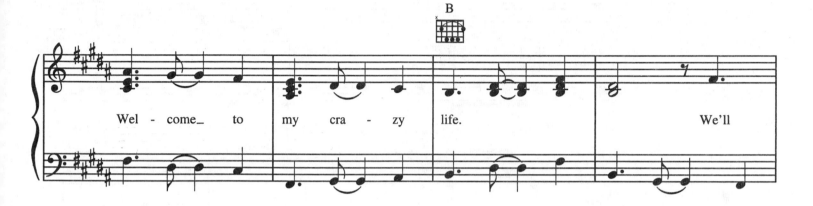

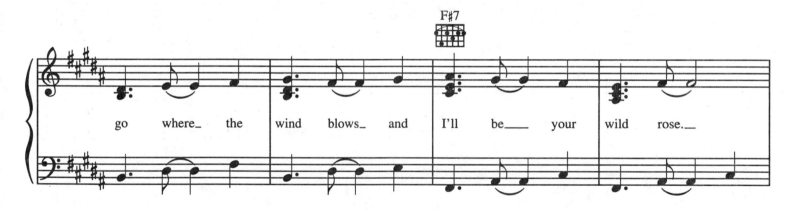

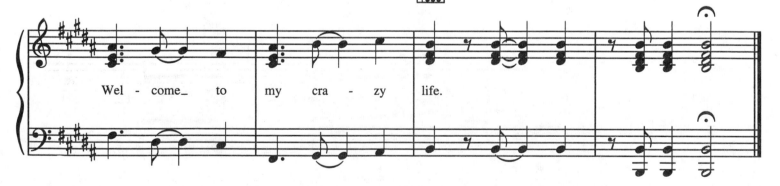

Verse 2:
Sweetheart, before this night is through,
I could fall in love with you.
Come dancin' on the edge with me,
Let my passion set you free.
(To Chorus:)

THE MOST BEAUTIFUL GIRL

Words and Music by
NORRIS WILSON, BILLY SHERRILL
and RORY BOURKE

The Most Beautiful Girl - 3 - 1

The Most Beautiful Girl - 3 - 2

The Most Beautiful Girl - 3 - 3

From the Twentieth Century-Fox Film "9 TO 5"

NINE TO FIVE

Words and Music by
DOLLY PARTON

Lyrics:

Tum-ble out of bed and stum-ble to the kitch-en; pour my-self a cup

2. (see additional lyrics)

of am-bi-tion, and yawn, and stretch, and try to come to life.

Jump in the show-er, and the blood starts pump-ing;

Nine To Five - 3 - 1

Verse 2:
They let you dream just to watch them shatter;
You're just a step on the boss man's ladder,
But you've got dreams he'll never take away.
In the same boat with a lot of your friends;
Waitin' for the day your ship'll come in,
And the tide's gonna turn, and it's all gonna roll your way.
(To Chorus:)

Chorus 4 , 6:
Nine to five, they've got you where they want you;
There's a better life, and you dream about it, don't you?
It's a rich man's game, no matter what they call it;
And you spend your life putting money in his pocket.

Nine To Five - 3 - 3

NO TIME TO KILL

By CLINT BLACK
and HAYDEN NICHOLAS

Bright country 2-beat ♩ = 96

Guitar (Capo 1st fret):

Keyboard:

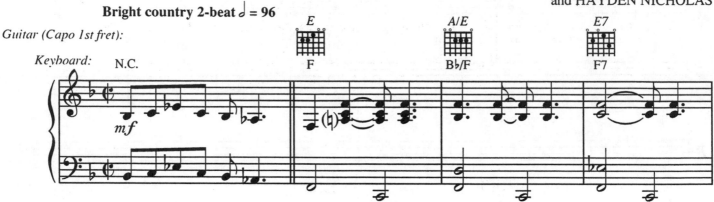

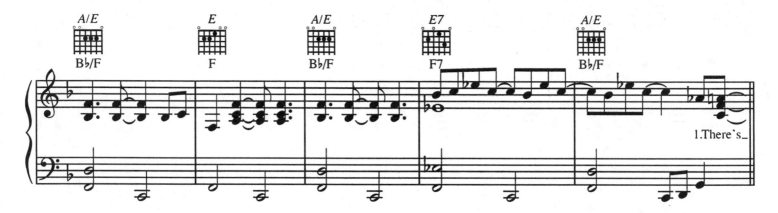

1.There's

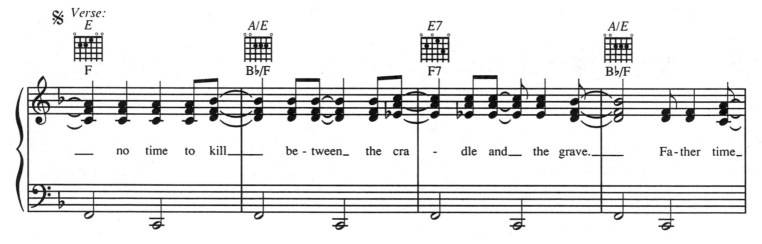

no time to kill__ be-tween__ the cra - dle and__ the grave.__ Fa-ther time__

still takes a toll__ on ev-'ry min-ute that__ you save.__ Le-gal ten-

No Time to Kill - 5 - 1

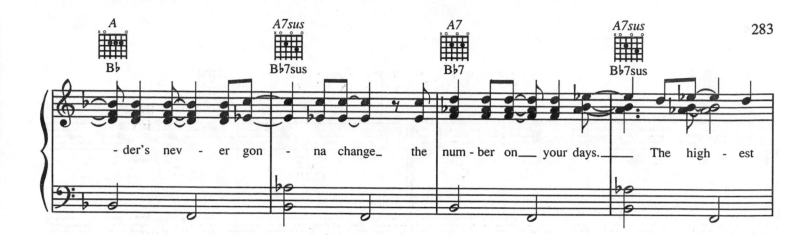

-der's nev - er gon - na change_ the num - ber on_ your days._ The high - est

cost of liv - in's dy - in', that's_ one ev - 'ry - bod - y pays._ So

have it spent_ be - fore_ you get the bill,_ there's no time_ to kill._

— 2. If we'd

D.S. 𝄋

No Time to Kill - 5 - 2

_No time to kill____ e - ven I've said__ it, and_

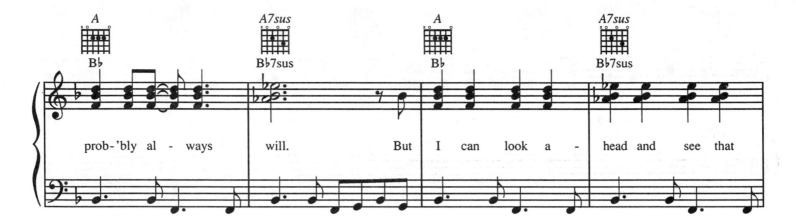

prob-'bly al - ways will. But I can look a - head and see that

_time ain't stand - in' still.___ No time__ to kill____ but time to change, the kind__ of_

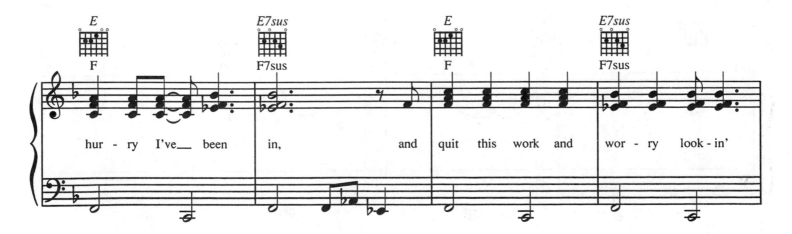

_hur - ry I've__ been in, and quit this work and wor - ry look-in'_

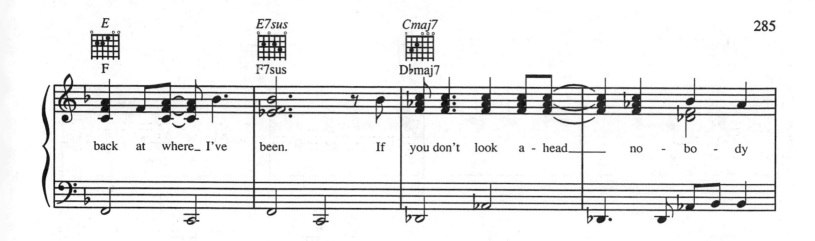

back at where_ I've been.   If   you don't look a-head___ no - bo - dy

will,   there's   no   time___ to   kill.___

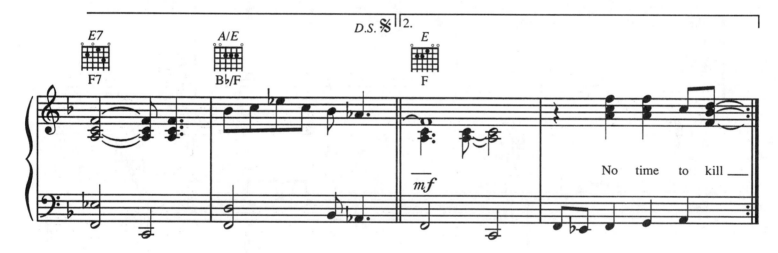

mf   No time to kill ___

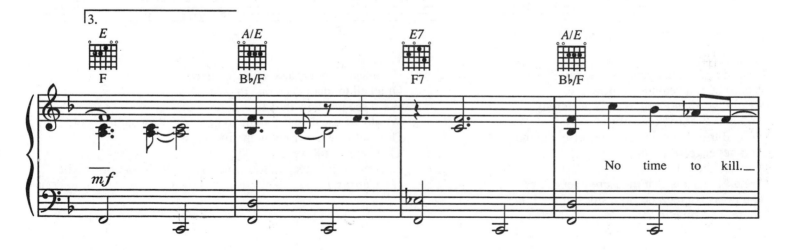

mf   No time to kill.___

No time to kill.

No time to kill.

Verse 2:
If we'd known ten years ago today
Would be ten years from now,
Would we spend tomorrow's yesterdays
And make it last some how,
Or lead the cheers in someone else's game,
And never learn to play,
And see the rules of thumb
Are all the same that measure every day?
The grass is green on both sides of the hill;
There's no time to kill.
(To Chorus:)

Verse 3:
If we had an hourglass, to watch each one go by,
Or a bell to mark each one to pass,
We'd see just how they fly.
Would we escalate the value to be worth its weight in gold
Or would we never know the fortunes
That we had till we grow old?
And do we just keep killin' time until there's no time to kill?
(To Chorus:)

ONE FRIEND

Words and Music by
DAN SEALS

One Friend - 3 - 1

One Friend - 3 - 2

one to tell it to... _____ If I had on - ly one friend left, I'd

want it to ___ be you.

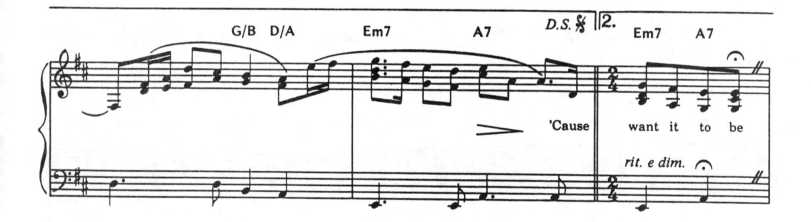

'Cause want it to be

rit. e dim.

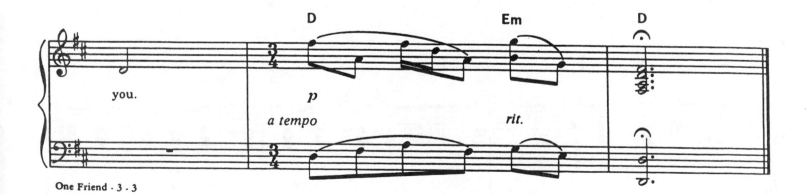

you.

p

a tempo

rit.

One Friend - 3 - 3

POCKET OF A CLOWN

Words and Music by
DWIGHT YOAKAM

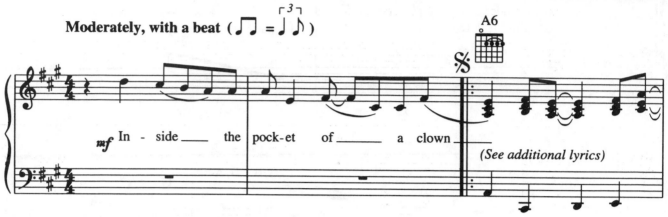

Pocket of a Clown - 3 - 1

To Coda ⊕

in - side ___ the pock - et of ___ a clown. ___

1.

Tacet

In - side ___ the heart-ache of ___ a fool ___

2.

D   A7/C#   D

A6

Hol - low lies ___   make a thin ___ dis - guise ___

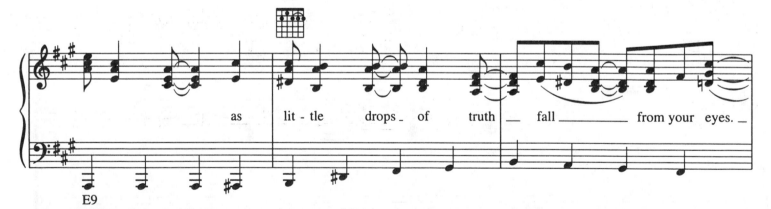

B9

as   lit - tle   drops ___ of   truth ___ fall ___ from your eyes. ___

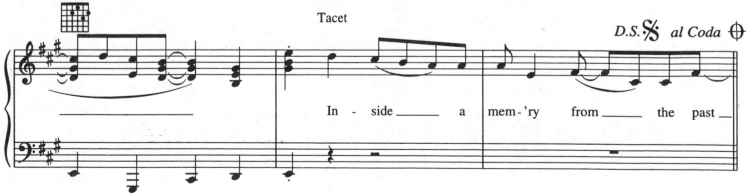

E9

Tacet

D.S. 𝄋 al Coda ⊕

In - side ___ a mem-'ry from ___ the past ___

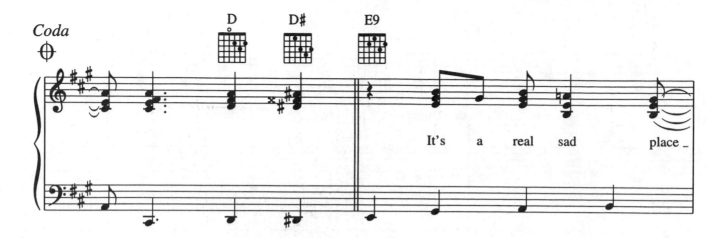

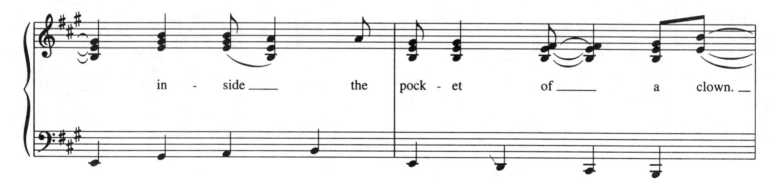

Additional lyrics

2. Inside the heartache of a fool
   You'll learn things they don't teach in school
   And lessons there can be real cruel
   Inside the heartache of a fool

3. Inside a memory from the past
   Lives every love that didn't last
   And sweet dreams can start to fade real fast
   Inside a memory from the past

RHINESTONE COWBOY

Words and Music by
LARRY WEISS

I've been walk- in' these streets__ so long__

sing - in' the same old song. I know ev - 'ry crack on these dir -

ty side-walks of Broad- way, where hus-tle is the name of the game__

Rhinestone Cowboy - 3 - 1

star spang-led ro-de-o. ___ Rhine-stone Cow-boy,

get-tin' cards and let-ters from peo-ple I don't ev-en know; ___

After 2nd time
repeat chorus and fade

of-fers com-ing o-ver the phone.

2. Well, I really don't mind the rain
   And a smile can hide the pain;
   But you're down when you're riding a train
   That's taking the long way . . .
   But I dream of the things I'll do
   With a subway token and a dollar
   Tucked inside my shoe . . .
   There's been a load of compromisin'
   On the road to my horizon;
   But I'm gonna be where the lights are shinin' on me . . .
   (Like a) . . .(to Chorus and fade)

Rhinestone Cowboy - 3 - 3

ROCKIN' YEARS

Words and Music by
FLOYD PARTON

Rockin' Years - 3 - 1

by you____ through our rock - in' years.____ Rock - in'

Chorus:

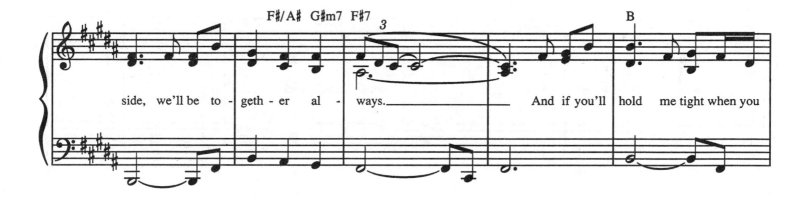

chairs, rock - in' ba - bies, rock - a - bye,____ rock of ag - es,____ side by

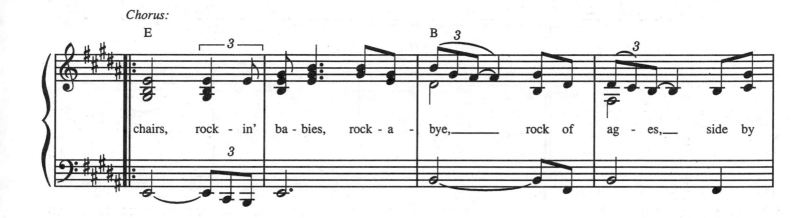

side, we'll be to - geth - er al - ways.____ And if you'll hold me tight when you

love me, that's all I'll____ ask of you. And I'll stand by you____

Verse 2:
I'll be your friend, I'll be your lover,
Until the end, there'll be no other,
And my heart has only room for one.
Yes, I'll always love you, and I'll always be here for you.
And I'll stand by you through our rockin' years.
(To Chorus:)

SNAP YOUR FINGERS

Moderate country shuffle ♩ = 108

Words and Music by
GRADY MARTIN and
ALEX ZINETIS

Snap Your Fingers - 3 - 1

run-ning. I'll be true,

To Coda ✛ | 1.

take a chance___ on me. Let your light turn

| 2.4. | *To next strain* ‖ 3.

door. *cresc.* Oh, I gain.

D.S. 𝄋 | *Bridge:*

had it, but I lost___ it. Now I've

got a bro-ken heart to mend. But I don't care what the

cost is. I've got to find my way back in. So you just snap your

So you just snap your

gain.

finger snaps

Verse 2:
Let your light turn green.
Baby I've gotta know.
Give me some kind of clue;
Should I stay or go?

Let me love you like the lover
That you used to know.
Turn the key and let me in
Through that same old door.
(To Bridge:)

On D.S. after Bridge both times:
So you just snap your fingers,
Baby, I'll come running.
I'll do anything
To get back again.

SOMEONE ELSE'S STAR

Words and Music by
SKIP EWING and JIM WEATHERLY

wish with all___ my___ might, for the love___ I'm___ dream-ing of and

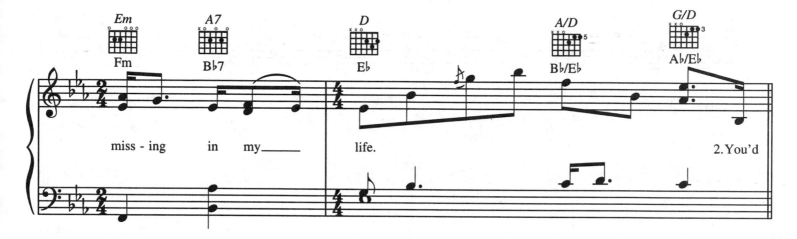

miss - ing in my_____ life. 2. You'd

Verse:

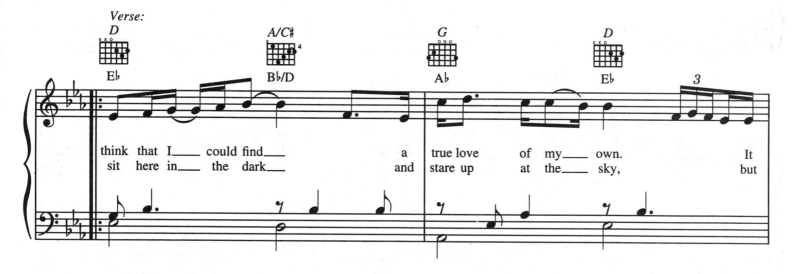

think that I___ could find___ a true love of my___ own. It

sit here in___ the dark___ and stare up at the___ sky, but

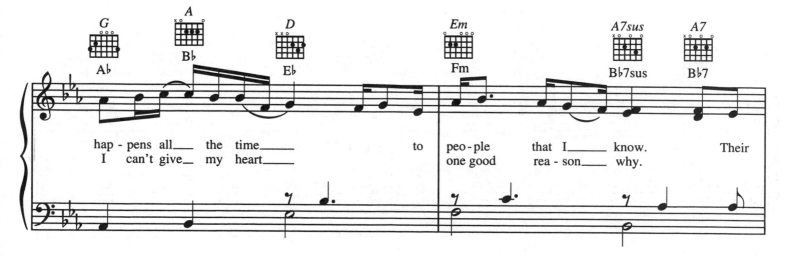

hap - pens all___ the time_____ to peo - ple that I_____ know. Their

I can't give___ my heart_____ one good rea - son___ why. Their

Someone Else's Star - 5 - 2

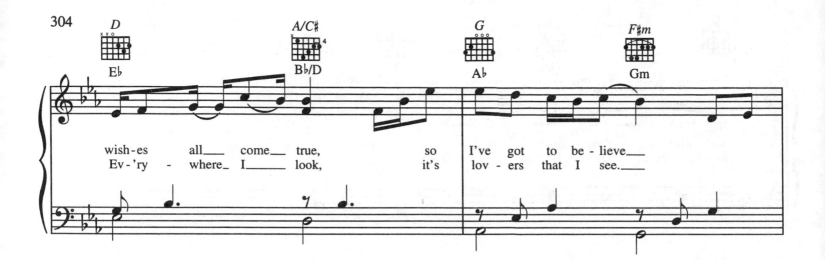

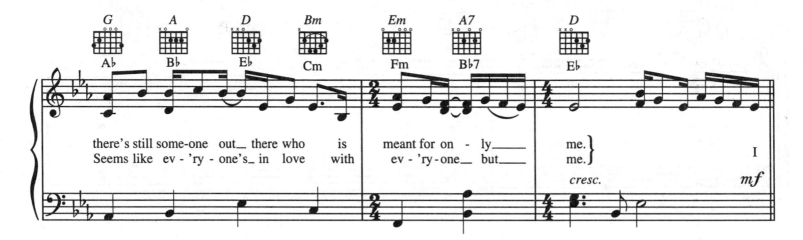

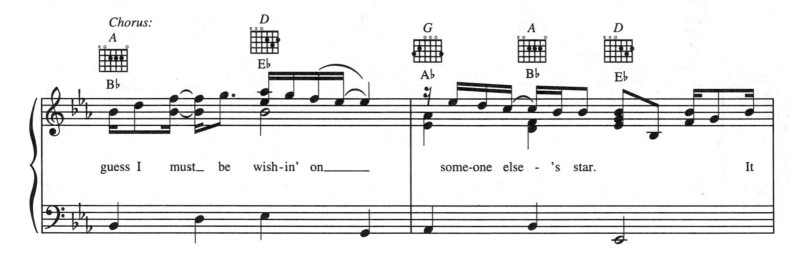

can't I be__ as luck-y as__ those oth-er peo-ple are?__ I

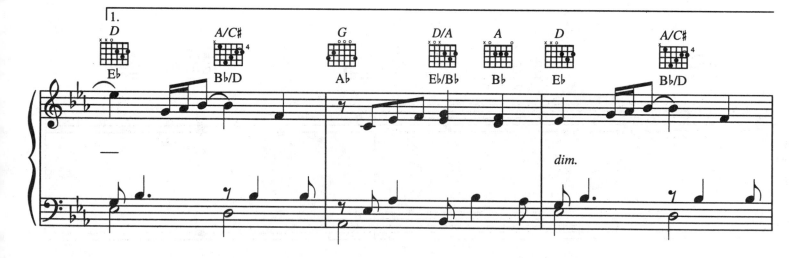

guess I must_ be__ wish-in' on some-one else-'s star.__

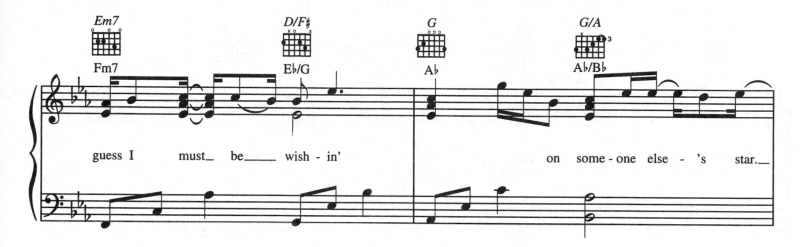

1.

dim.

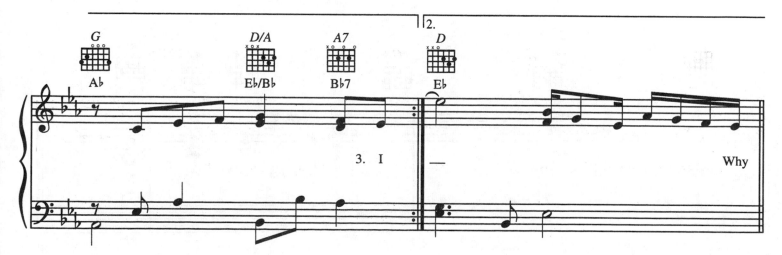

3. I __ Why

2.

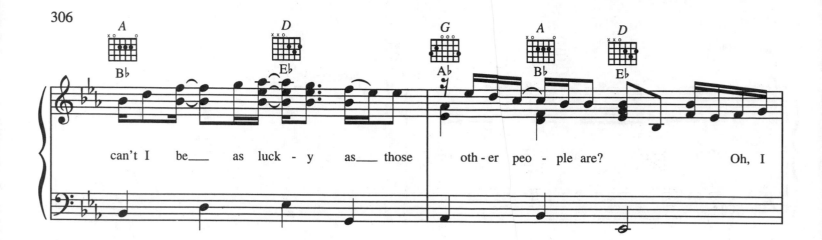

can't I be___ as luck-y as___ those oth-er peo-ple are? Oh, I

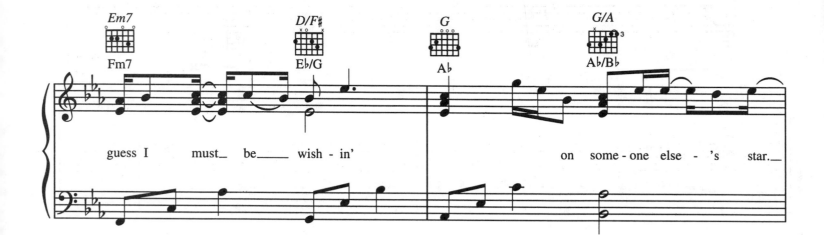

guess I must_ be___ wish-in' on some-one else-'s star.___

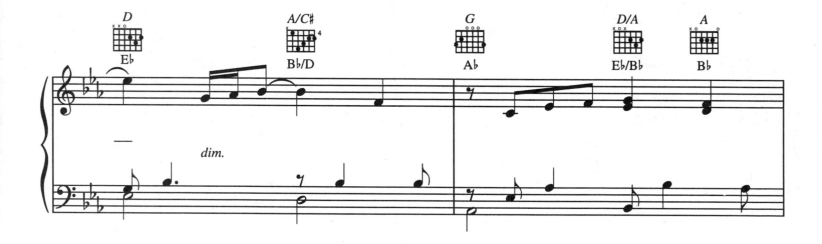

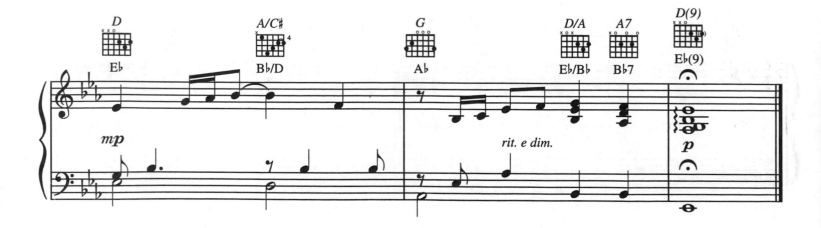

SOMETHING IN RED

Words and Music by
ANGELA KASET

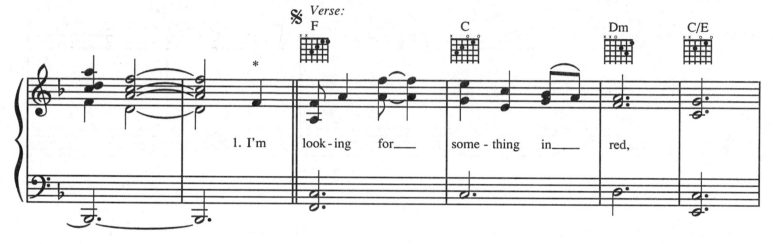

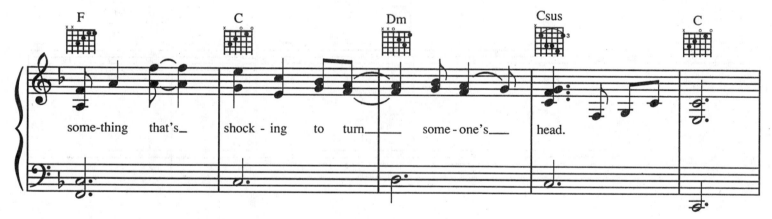

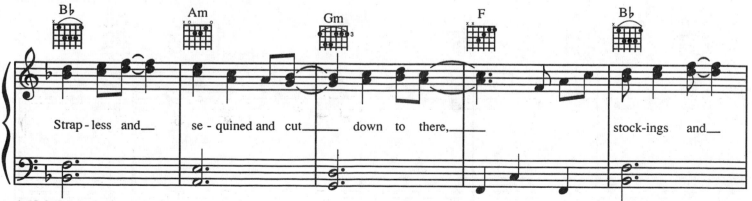

Melody sung one octave lower

Something in Red - 3 - 1

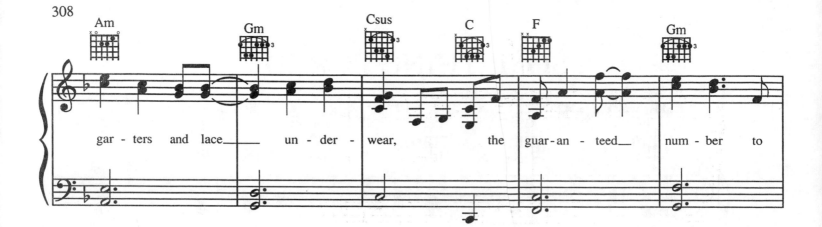

garters and lace__ un-der-wear, the guar-an-teed__ num-ber to

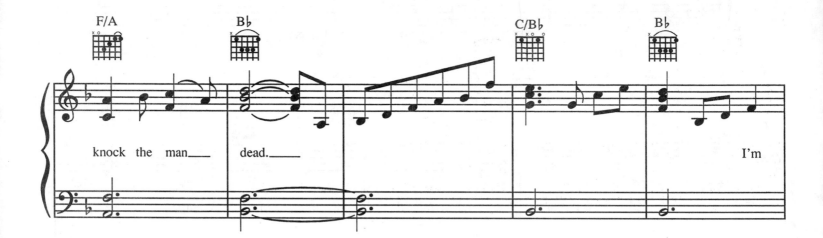

knock the man__ dead.__ I'm

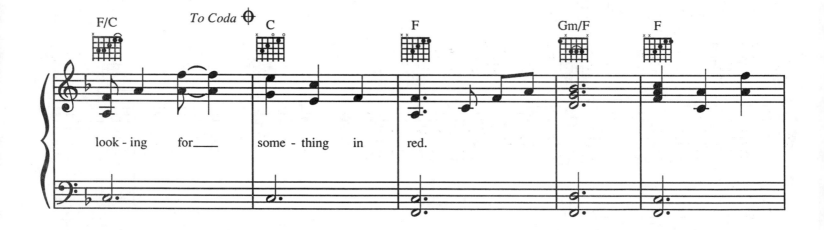

look-ing for__ some-thing in red.

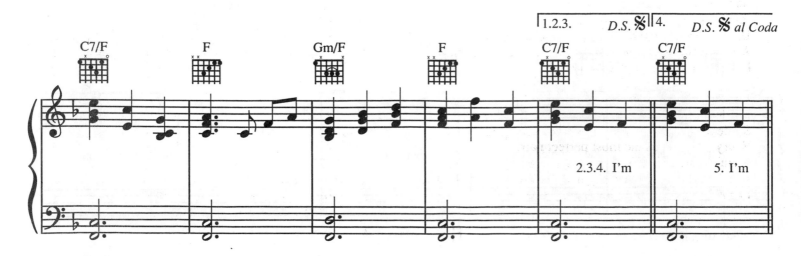

2.3.4. I'm 5. I'm

⊕ *Coda*

some - thing, I've got - ta have___ some - thing, I'm look - ing for___

some - thing___ in red.___

rit.   *a tempo*

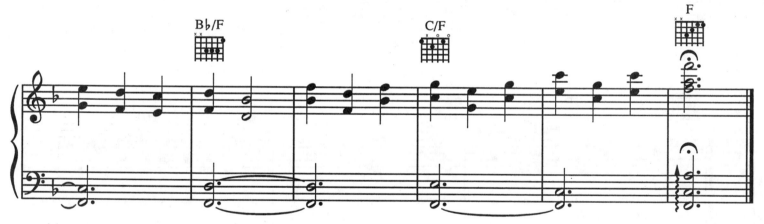

Verse 2:
I'm looking for something in green,
Something to outdo an ex-high school queen.
Jealousy comes in the color of jade.
Do you have some pumps and purse in this shade,
And a perfume that whispers "Please come back to me"?
I'm looking for something in green.

Verse 3:
I'm looking for something in white,
Something that shimmers in soft candlelight.
Everyone calls us the most perfect pair.
Should I wear a veil or a rose in my hair?
Well, the train must be long and the waist must be tight.
I'm looking for something in white.

Verse 4:
I'm looking for something in blue,
Something real tiny, the baby's brand new.
He has his father's nose and his chin.
We once were hot lovers, now we're more like friends.
Don't tell me that's just what old married folk do.
I'm looking for something in blue.

Verse 5:
I'm looking for something in red,
Like the one that I wore when I first turned his head.
Strapless and sequined and cut down to there,
Just a size larger than I wore last year,
The guaranteed number to knock the man dead.
I'm looking for something,
I've gotta have something,
I'm looking for something in red.

SOUTHERN GRACE

Written by
PORTER HOWELL, BRADY SEALS
and STEWART HARRIS

Slowly ♩ = 64

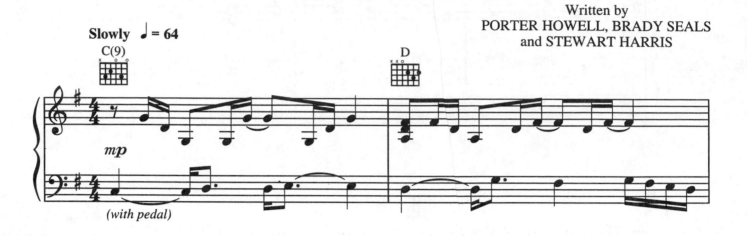

Verse:

1. First time I felt the mag - ic___ of her kiss___ was un-der a Car - o - li-na moon.___
2. *See additional lyrics*

_____ Sweet South-ern style,_____ ten-der but a lit-tle wild.___ For

Southern Grace - 5 - 1

me no oth-er love will ev-er do.___ Her

cresc.

Chorus:

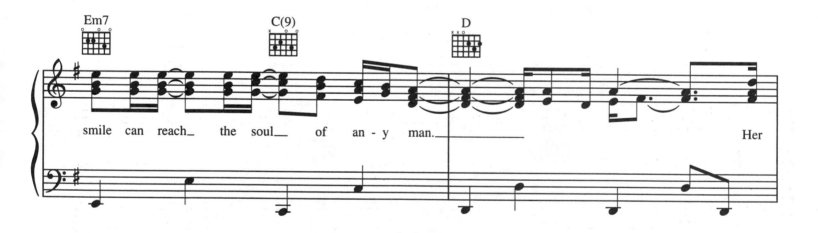

voice is like___ the whis-per of a warm wind through the pines.___ Her

f

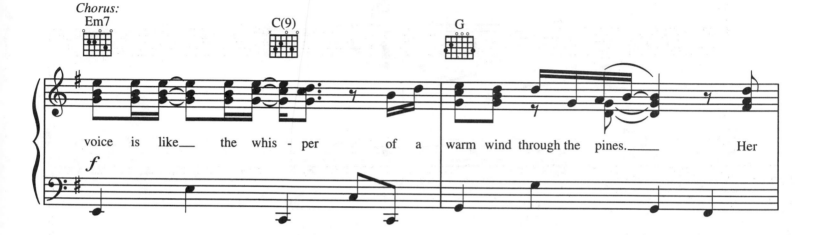

smile can reach___ the soul___ of an-y man.___ Her

heart is strong,___ her love is true,___ and her touch is soft___ as lace.___ There ain't noth-

dim.

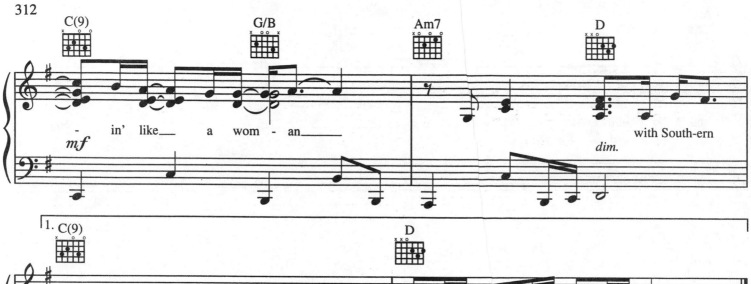

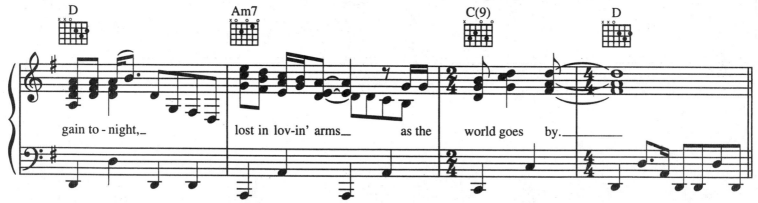

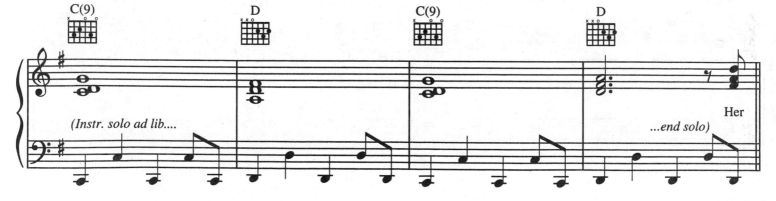

Chorus:

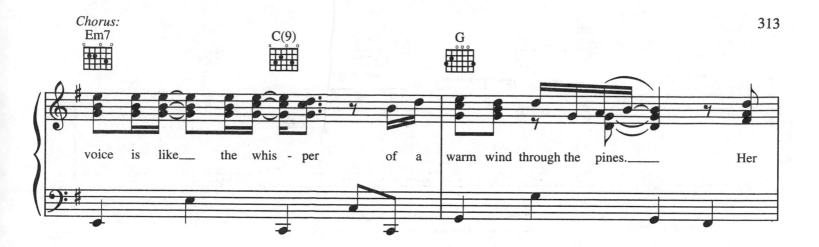

voice is like__ the whis - per of a warm wind through the pines.__ Her

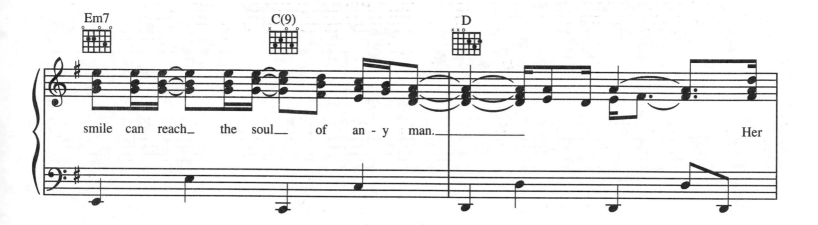

smile can reach__ the soul__ of an - y man.__ Her

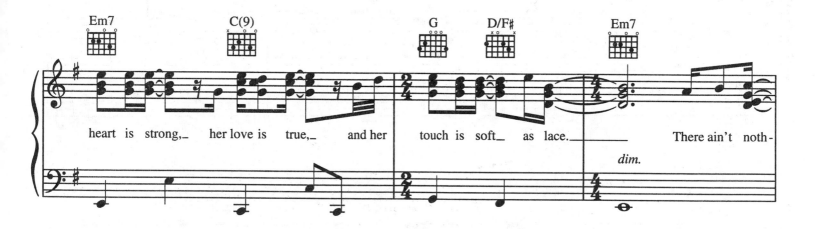

heart is strong,__ her love is true,__ and her touch is soft__ as lace.__ There ain't noth-

- in' like__ a wom - an,__ there ain't noth - in' like__ a wom - an,__

no there ain't noth - in' like_ my_ wom - an,_

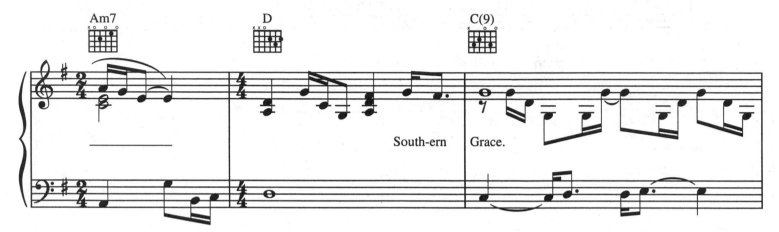

South-ern Grace.

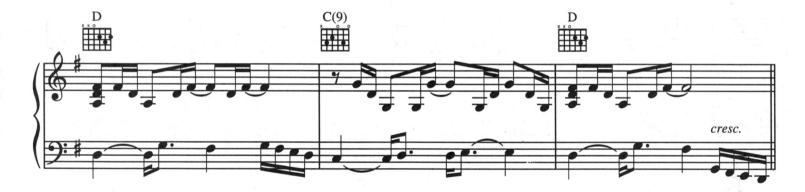

cresc.

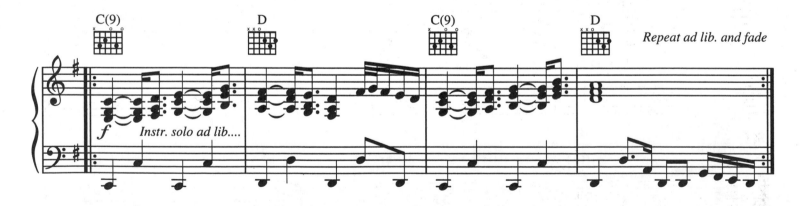

Repeat ad lib. and fade

f *Instr. solo ad lib....*

Verse 2:
You should see the way she walks into a room;
It's almost like her feet don't touch the floor.
But when the chips are down, her feet are firmly on the ground.
I could never ask for any more.
(To Chorus:)

TAKE ME AS I AM

Two beat ♩ = 76

Words and Music by
BOB DIPIERO and KAREN STALEY

Take Me As I Am - 3 - 1

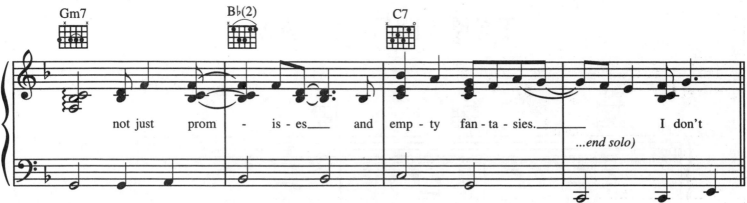

not just prom - is - es___ and emp - ty fan - ta - sies.___ I don't
...end solo)

Chorus:

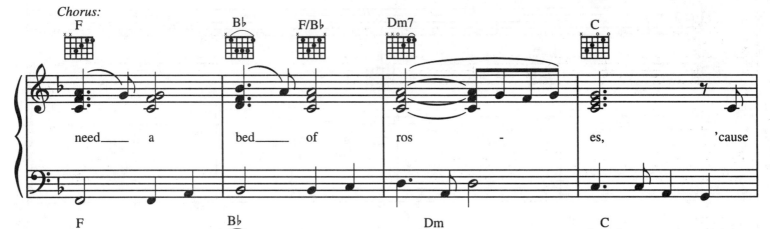

need___ a bed___ of ros - es, 'cause

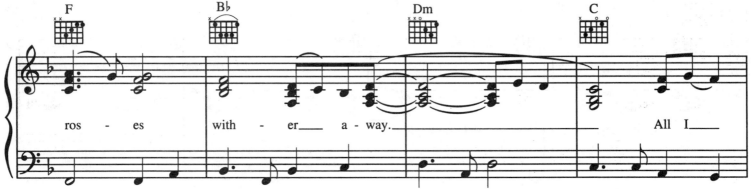

ros - es with - er___ a - way.___ All I___

real - ly need is hon - es - ty___

___ from some-one with a strong_ heart, a gen - tle hand,___

Verse 2:
Baby, I need for you to know
Just exactly how I feel.
Fiery passions come and go.
I'd trade a million pretty words
For one touch that is real.
(To Chorus:)

THANK GOD FOR KIDS

Words and Music by
EDDY RAVEN

Thank God For Kids - 3 - 1

Thank God For Kids - 3 - 2

VERSE II

"Daddy, how does this thing fly?"
And a hundred other wheres and whys
You really don't know but you try
THANK GOD FOR KIDS
When you look down in those trusting eyes
That look to you, you realize
There's a love that you can't buy
THANK GOD FOR KIDS

TO ME

Words and Music by
MACK DAVID and
MIKE REID

To Me - 3 - 1

Just as

cresc.

Coda

to   me.

rall.   p   mp

a tempo

dim. e rit.

To Me - 3 - 3

TWO SPARROWS IN A HURRICANE

Words and Music by
MARK ALAN SPRINGER

*Sing melody one octave lower.
**Play chord in parentheses 2nd time only.

Two Sparrows in a Hurricane - 5 - 1

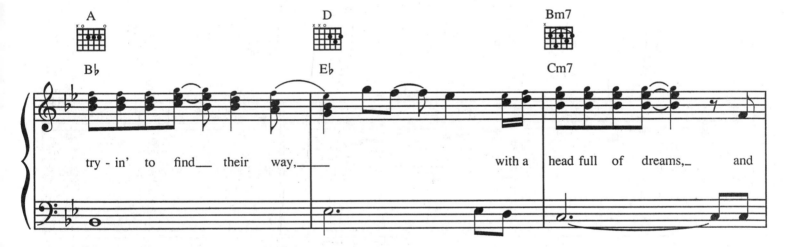

Chorus:

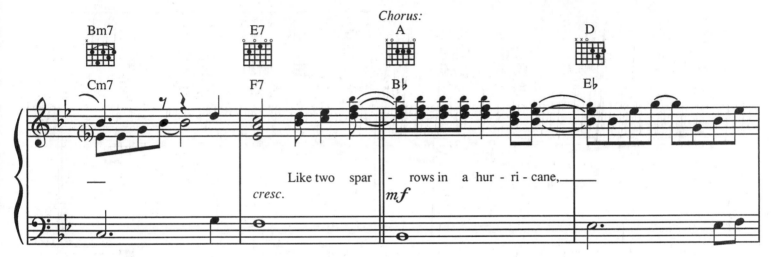

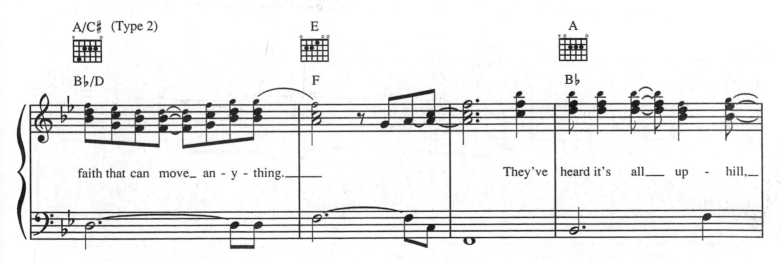

but all they know is how they feel. The world says they'll nev - er make

it; love says they will.

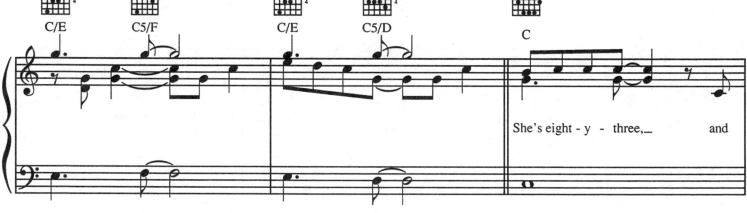

She's eight - y - three, and

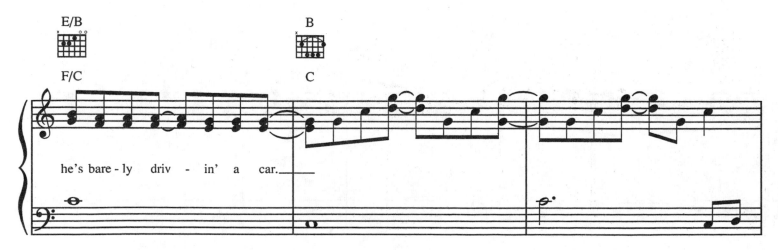

he's bare - ly driv - in' a car.

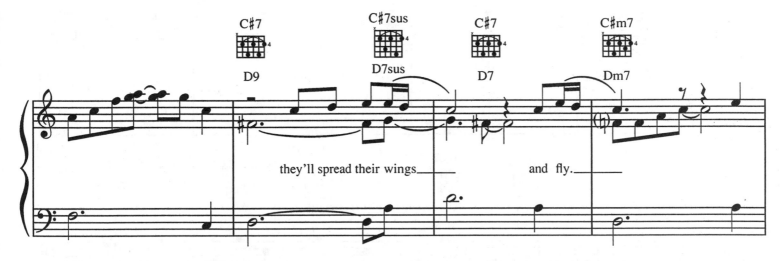

Two Sparrows in a Hurricane - 5 - 4

Verse 2:
There's a baby cryin', and one more on the way.
There's a wolf at the door with a big stack of bills they can't pay.
The clouds are dark, and the wind is high,
But they can see the other side.
(To Chorus:)

THE VOWS GO UNBROKEN
(Always True to You)

Words and Music by
GARY BURR and ERIC KAZ

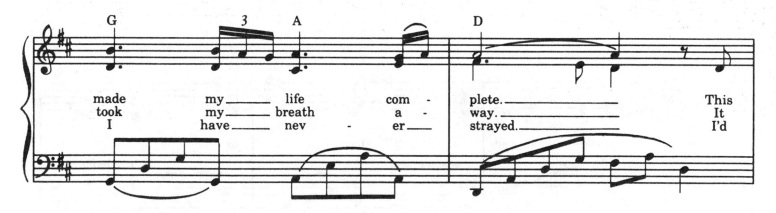

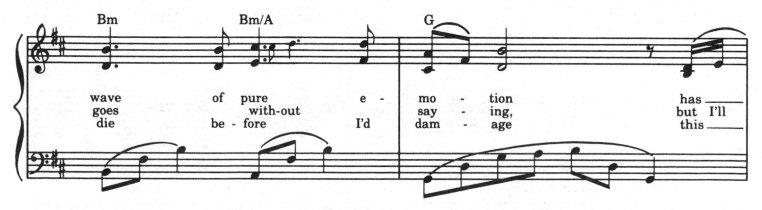

The Vows Go Unbroken - 3 - 1

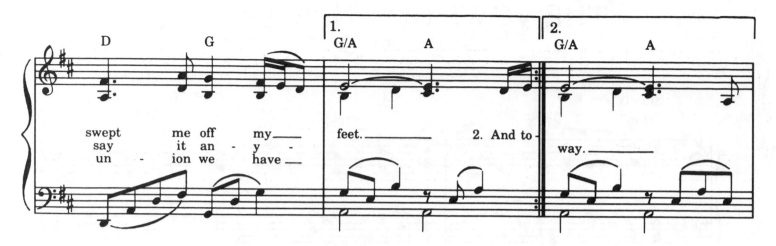

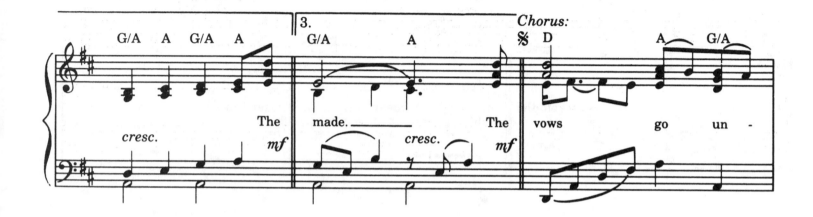

The Vows Go Unbroken - 3 - 3

WHOSE BED HAVE YOUR BOOTS BEEN UNDER?

Words and Music by SHANIA TWAIN
and ROBERT JOHN "MUTT" LANGE

Bright shuffle ♩ = 112

Whose bed have your boots been un - der?

Chorus:

Whose bed have your boots been un - der?___ And whose heart did you steal, I won - der?___

This time___ did it feel like thun - der, ba - by? Well, whose bed have your

boots been un - der?___ 1. Don't look so

(Spoken:) Come on boots . . .

(Instrumental solo ad lib. . . .

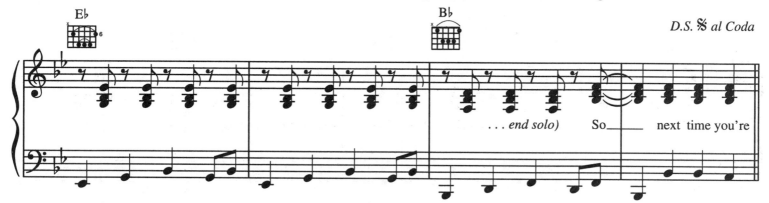

D.S. 𝄋 al Coda

. . . end solo) So___ next time you're

⊕ Coda

feel like thun - der.   Whose bed have your boots been un - der?___

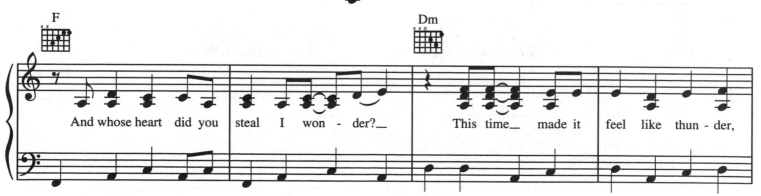

And whose heart did you steal I won - der?___   This time___ made it feel like thun - der,

Verse 2:
I heard you've been sneakin'
Around with Jill.
And what about that weekend
With Beverly Hill?
And I've seen you walkin'
With long-legs Louise.
And you weren't just talkin'
Last night with Denise.
(To Chorus:)

Additional lyrics for D.S.:
So next time you're lonely,
Don't call on me.
Try the operator,
Maybe she'll be free.
(To Chorus:)

From the Original Motion Picture Soundtrack "BEACHES"

THE WIND BENEATH MY WINGS

Words and Music by
LARRY HENLEY and **JEFF SILBAR**

It must have been cold there in my shad - ow,___

to nev - er have sun - light on your

The Wind beneath My Wings - 7 - 1

THE RED STROKES

By
JAMES GARVER, LISA SANDERSON,
JENNY YATES and GARTH BROOKS

L.H. tacet 1st Verse on recording.

The Red Strokes - 4 - 1

Chorus:

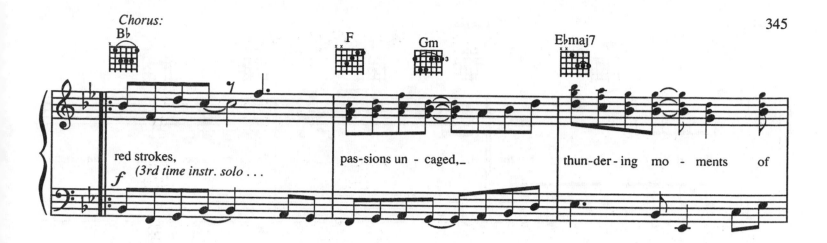

red strokes, *(3rd time instr. solo . . .* pas-sions un - caged,___ thun-der-ing mo - ments of

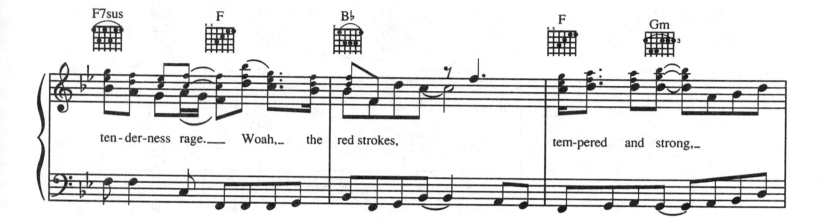

ten-der-ness rage.___ Woah,___ the red strokes, tem-pered and strong,___

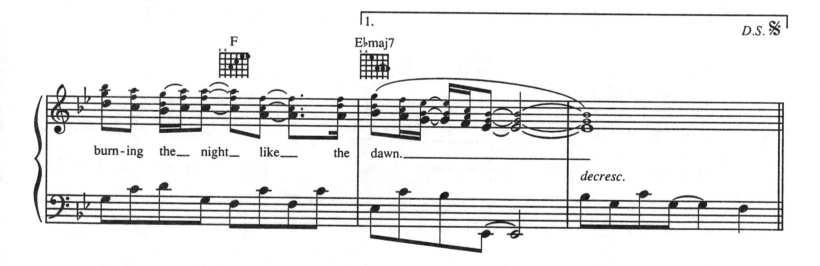

burn-ing the___ night___ like___ the dawn.

D.S. 𝄋

decresc.

dawn.___

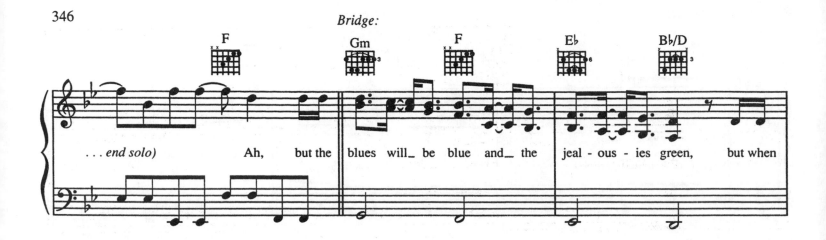

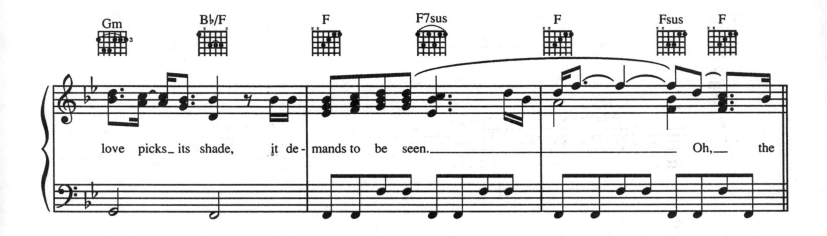

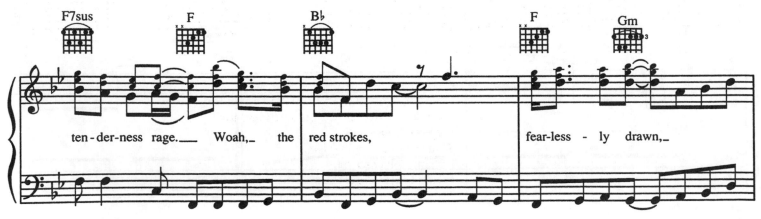

burn-ing the night___ like___ the dawn._____ Oh,___ the

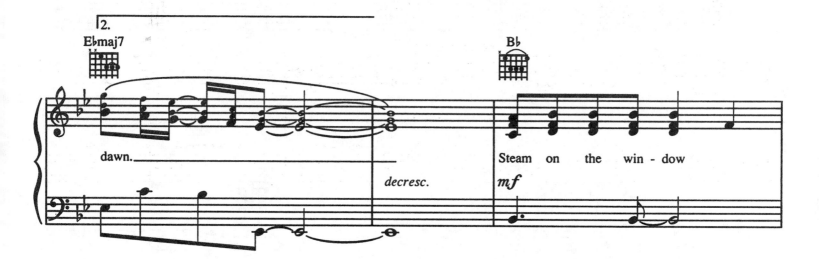

dawn._____ *decresc.* Steam on the win - dow *mf*

salt in a kiss,___ two hearts have nev - er pound-ed like___ this.

rit. poco a poco

Verse 2:
Steam on the window, Salt in a kiss:
Two hearts have never pounded like this.
Inspired by a vision
That they can't command,
Erasing the borders
With each brush of a hand.
(To Chorus:)

RODEO

Words and Music by
LARRY B. BASTIAN

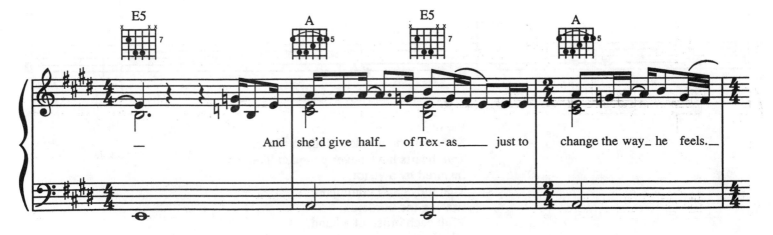

Rodeo - 4 - 1

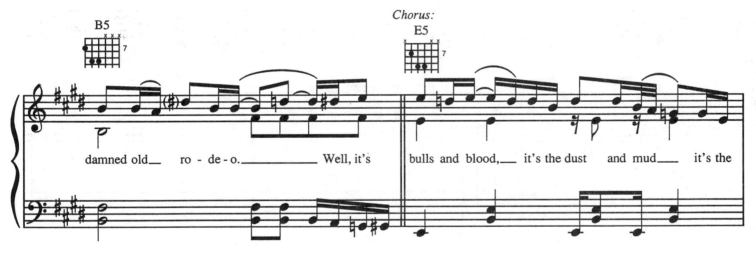

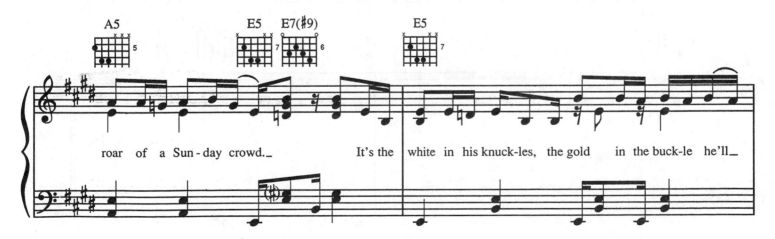

Rodeo - 4 - 2

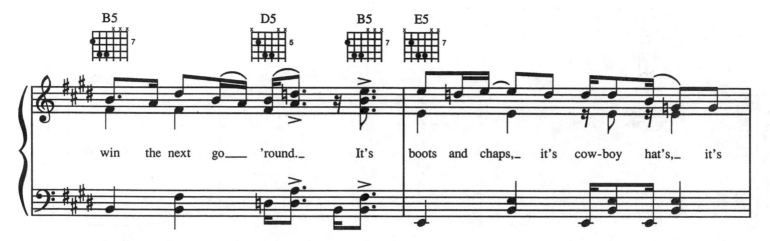

win the next go___ 'round._ It's boots and chaps,_ it's cow-boy hat's,_ it's

spurs and_ lat-i-go.___ It's the ropes___and the reins,_ and the joy_ and the pain,_ and they call_

_ the thing ro - de-o.___

2. She ___
3. It'll ___

Rodeo - 4 - 3

It's the broncs___ and the blood,_ it's the steers_ and the mud,_ and they call___

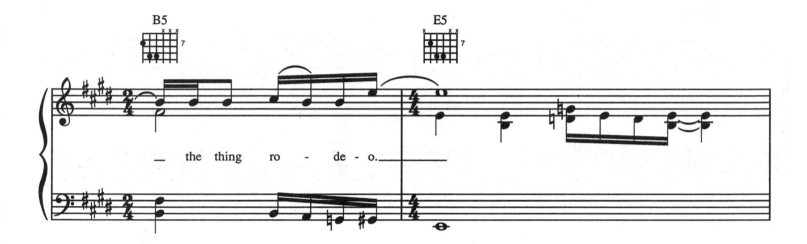

_ the thing ro - de - o.___

Intsrumental solo . . .

Verse 2:
She does her best to hold him
When his love comes to call.
But his need for it controls him
And her back's against the wall.
And it's "So long, girl, I'll see you.",
When it's time for him to go.
You know the woman wants her cowboy
Like he wants his rodeo.
(To Chorus:)

Verse 3:
It'll drive a cowboy crazy,
It'll drive the man insane.
And he'll sell off everything he owns
Just to pay to play her game.
And a broken home and some broken bones
Is all he'll have to show
For all the years that he spent chasin'
This dream they call rodeo.
(To Chorus:)

THE THUNDER ROLLS

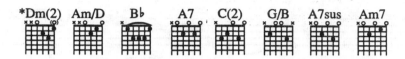

*Alternate between E and F on the 1st string.

Words and Music by
GARTH BROOKS and
PAT ALGER

Slow rock ♩ = 84

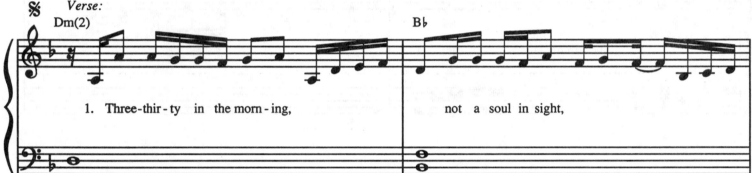

with pedal

Verse:

1. Three-thir-ty in the morn-ing, not a soul in sight,

the cit-y's look-in' like a ghost town on a moon-less sum-mer night.

Rain-drops on the wind-shield, there's a storm mov-ing in.

The Thunder Rolls - 4 - 1

He's head - in' back from some - where____ that he nev - er should_ have been.__

And the thun - der rolls,____

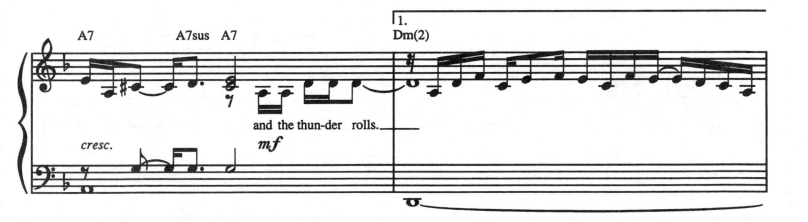

and the thun - der rolls.____

The thun - der

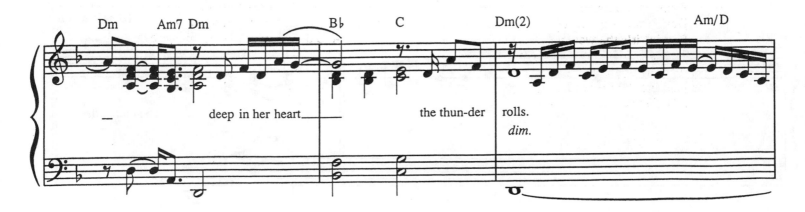

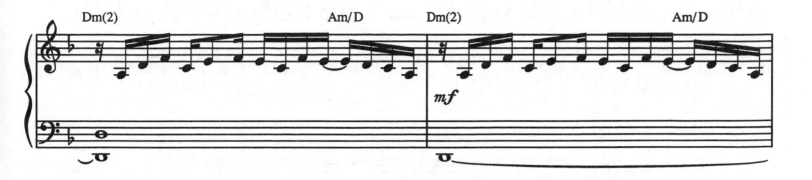

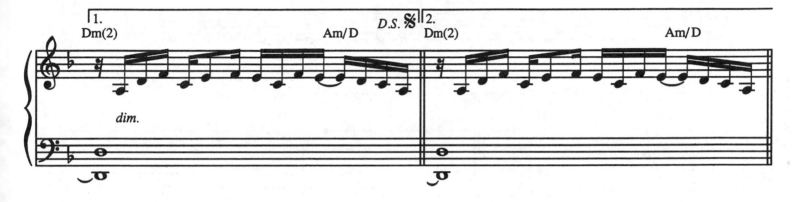

Repeat ad lib. and fade

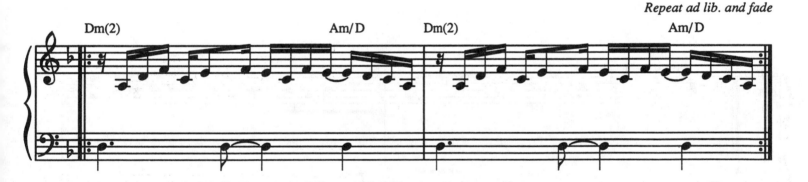

Verse 2:
Every light is burnin'
In a house across town.
She's pacin' by the telephone
In her faded flannel gown,
Askin' for a miracle,
Hopin' she's not right.
Prayin' it's the weather
That's kept him out all night.
And the thunder rolls,
And the thunder rolls.
(To Chorus:)

Verse 3:
She's waitin' by the window
When he pulls into the drive.
She rushes out to hold him,
Thankful he's alive.
But on the wind and rain
A strange new perfume blows,
And the lightnin' flashes in her eyes,
And he knows that she knows.
And the thunder rolls,
And the thunder rolls.
(To Chorus:)

AIN'T GOING DOWN ('TIL THE SUN COMES UP)

Words and Music by
KENT BLAZY, KIM WILLIAMS and
GARTH BROOKS

Rock ♩ = 168

Verse 1 & 2:

1. Six o'-clock on Fri-day eve-ning, Ma-ma does-n't know she's leav-ing

'til she hears the screen door slam-ming, rub-ber squeal-in', gears a-jam-ming.

Ain't Going Down ('til the Sun Comes Up) - 5 - 1

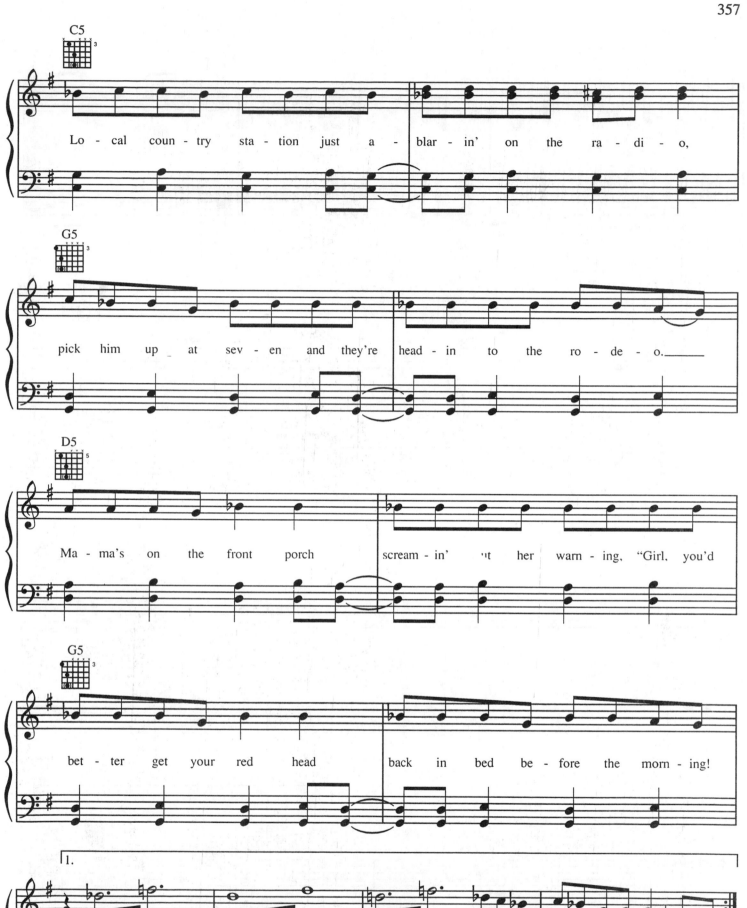

Lo - cal coun - try sta - tion just a - blar - in' on the ra - di - o,

pick him up at sev - en and they're head - in to the ro - de - o._____

Ma - ma's on the front porch scream - in' 't her warn - ing, "Girl, you'd

bet - ter get your red head back in bed be - fore the morn - ing!

358

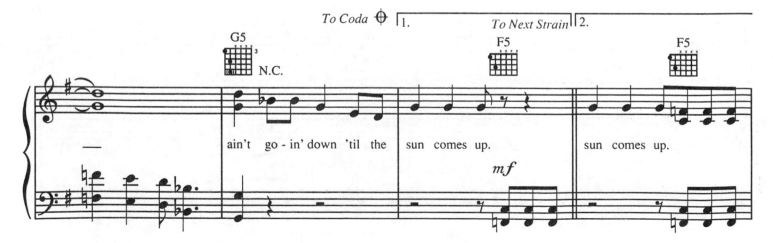

Ain't Going Down ('til the Sun Comes Up) - 5 - 3

Verse 3 & 4:

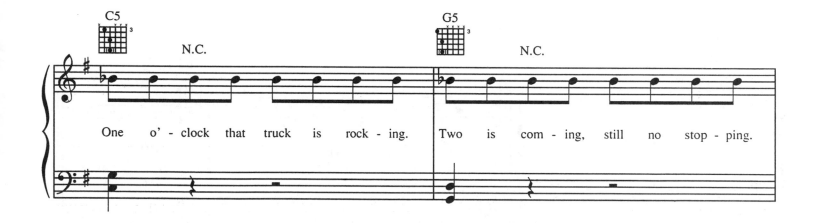

3. Ten 'til twelve is wine and danc - ing. Mid - night starts the hard ro - manc - ing.

One o' - clock that truck is rock - ing. Two is com - ing, still no stop - ping.

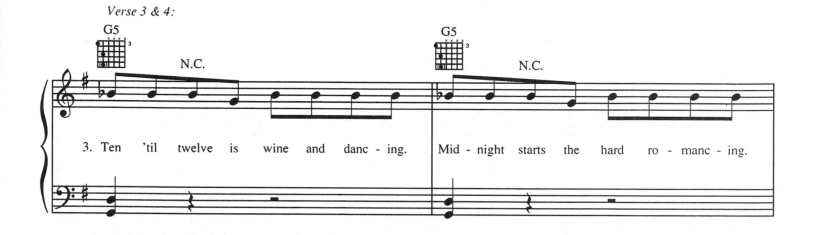

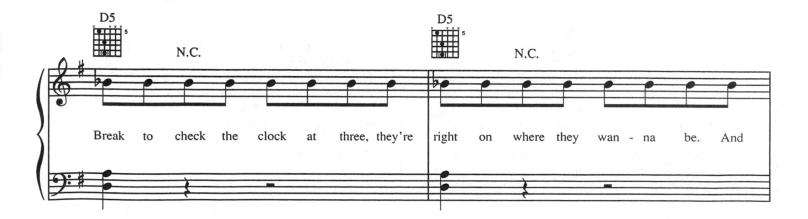

Break to check the clock at three, they're right on where they wan - na be. And

Ain't Going Down ('til the Sun Comes Up) - 5 - 4

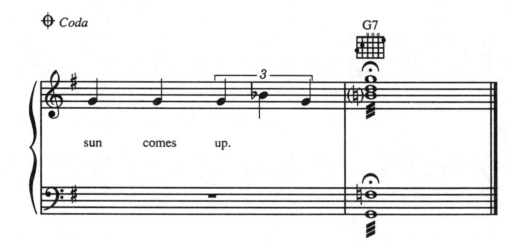

Verse 2:
Nine o'clock the show is ending,
But the fun is just beginning.
She knows he's anticipating
But she's gonna keep him waiting.
Grab a bite to eat
And then they're headin' to the honky tonk,
But loud crowds and line dancing
Just ain't what they really want.
Drive out to the boondocks and park down by the creek,
And where it's George Strait 'til real late
And dancing cheek to cheek.
(To Chorus:)

Verse 4:
Six o'clock on Saturday
Her folks don't know he's on his way.
The stalls are clean, the horses fed,
They say she's grounded 'til she's dead.
And here he comes around the bend,
Slowing down, she's jumping in.
Hey, Mom! Your daughter's gone
And there they go again. Hey!
(To Chorus:)

THE DANCE

Words and Music by
TONY ARATA

Slowly ♩ = 68
N.C.

with Pedal

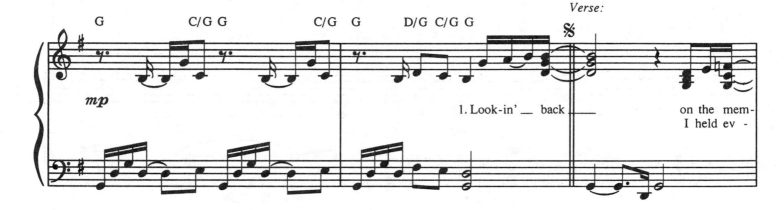

G   C/G G   C/G G   D/G C/G G   *Verse:*

mp

1. Look-in' __ back __ on the mem-
   I held ev -

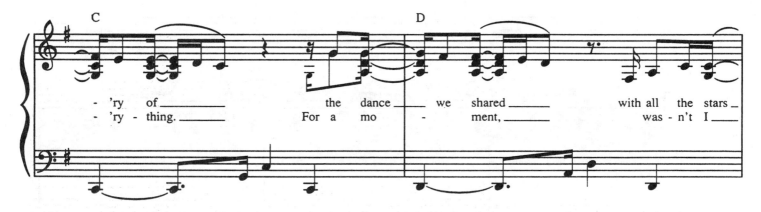

C

D

- 'ry of _____ the dance __ we shared _____ with all the stars_
- 'ry - thing. _____ For a mo - ment, _____ was - n't I __

G   D   G

__ a - bove. __ For a mo - ment, __ all the world_
__ the king? __ If I'd on - ly known __ how the king__

The Dance - 3 - 1

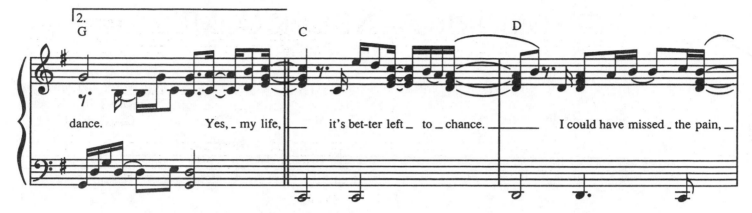

dance. Yes, _ my life, _____ it's bet-ter left _ to _ chance. _____ I could have missed _ the pain, _

_____ but I'd have had _ to _ miss _____ the _____ dance.

rit. *a tempo*

mp

Repeat ad lib. and fade

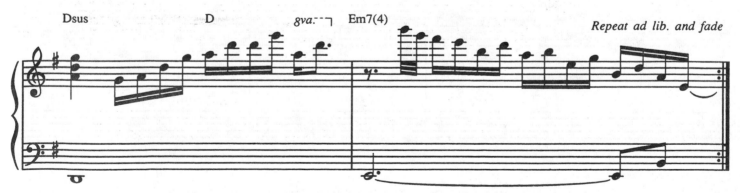

The Dance - 3 - 3

IF TOMORROW NEVER COMES

Words and Music by
KENT BLAZY and
GARTH BROOKS

If Tomorrow Never Comes - 3 - 1

would she ev-er doubt ___ the way ___ I feel ___ a-bout ___ her in ___ my

Chorus:

heart. ___ If to-mor-row nev-er comes, will she know how much I

loved her? ___ Did I try in ev-ery way ___ to show her ev-ery-day ___

___ that she's my on-ly one? ___ And if my time on ___ earth ___ were

through, ___ and she must face ___ this world with-out me, ___

If Tomorrow Never Comes - 3 - 2

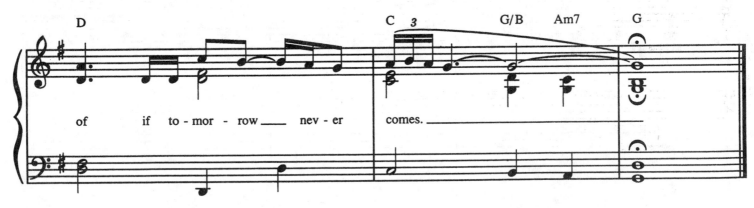

Verse 2:
'Cause I've lost loved ones in my life.
Who never knew how much I loved them.
Now I live with the regret
That my true feelings for them never were revealed.
So I made a promise to myself
To say each day how much she means to me
And avoid that circumstance
Where there's no second chance to tell her how I feel. ('Cause)
(To Chorus:)

THE RIVER

Words and Music by
GARTH BROOKS and VICTORIA SHAW

Slowly ♩ = 76

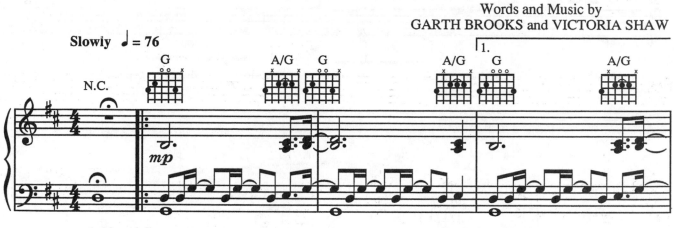

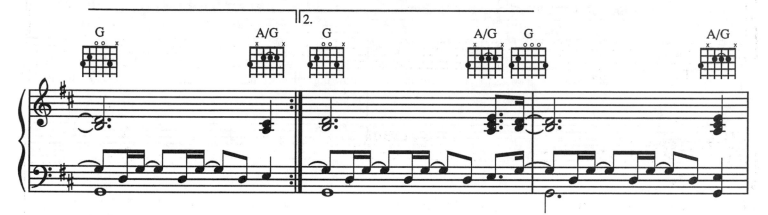

1. You know a

dream is like___ a riv - er, ev - er chang - in' as___ it flows. And the

The River - 5 - 1

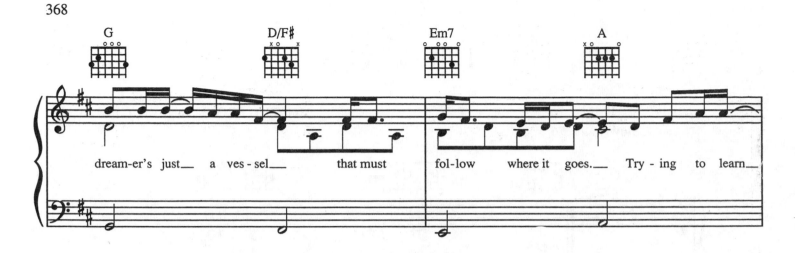

dream-er's just_ a ves-sel_ that must fol-low where it goes._ Try-ing to learn_

_ from what's_ be-hind you,_ and nev-er know-ing what's_ in_ store_ makes_ each day_

_ a con-stant bat-tle just to stay be-tween_ the shores._

cresc. **mf** And I will

Chorus:

sail my ves - sel 'til the riv - er runs_ dry. Like a

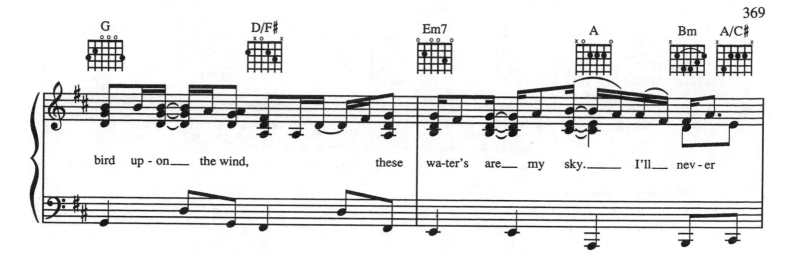

bird up-on___ the wind,   these wa-ter's are___ my sky.___ I'll___ nev-er

reach my des - ti-na-tion   if I nev-er try. So, I will___

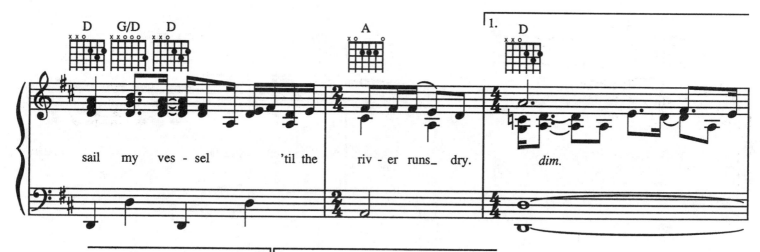

sail my ves - sel   'til the riv-er runs___ dry.   *dim.*

D.S. 𝄋

2. Too man-y   And there's bound to be___ rough__ wa-ters___ and I

know I'll take__ some falls._____ But with the Good Lord__ as__ my cap - tain, I____ can

make it through__ them all._____ Yes, I will sail my ves - sel 'til the

river runs____ dry. Like a bird up - on__ the wind, these

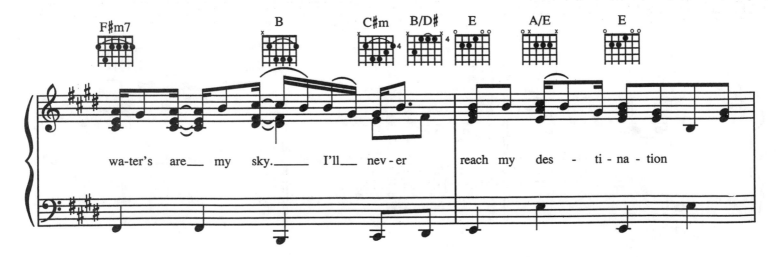

wa - ter's are__ my sky.____ I'll__ nev - er reach my des - ti - na - tion

Verse 2:
Too many times we stand aside
And let the waters slip away
'Til what we put off 'til tomorrow
Has now become today.
So, don't you sit upon the shoreline
And say you're satisfied.
Choose to chance the rapids
And dare to dance the tide. Yes, I will . . .
(To Chorus:)

The River - 5 - 5

STANDING OUTSIDE THE FIRE

By
JENNY YATES and GARTH BROOKS

*L.H. tacet verses 1 & 2 on recording.
**Chords in parentheses are played 2nd time only.

Standing Outside the Fire - 5 - 1

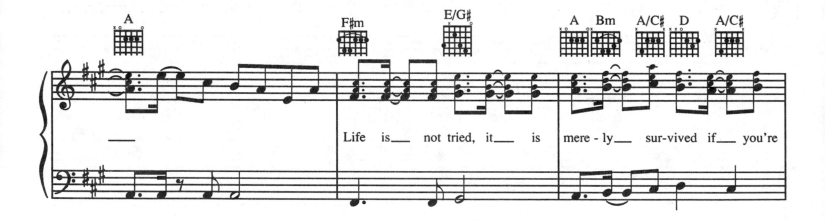

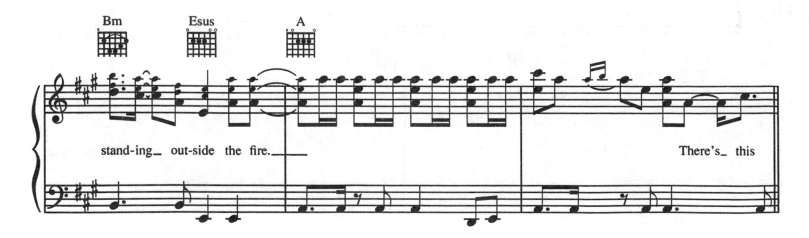

love that___ is burn-ing   deep in___ my soul,___   con - stant - ly yearn-ing to get

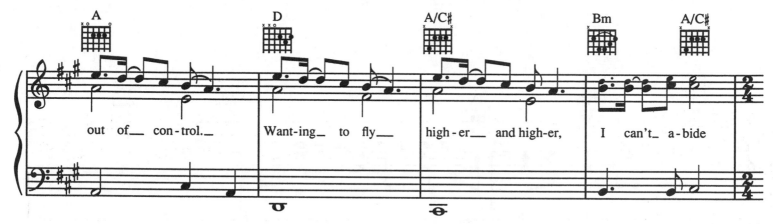

out of___ con-trol.___   Want-ing___ to fly___   high-er___ and high-er,   I   can't___ a-bide

stand - ing___ out -side_____ the fire.___   (Percussion break)

Chorus:

Stand-ing___ out-side the fire.___   Stand-ing___ out-side the fire.___

Life is___ not tried, it___ is   mere-ly___ sur-vived if___ you're stand - ing out-side the fire.___

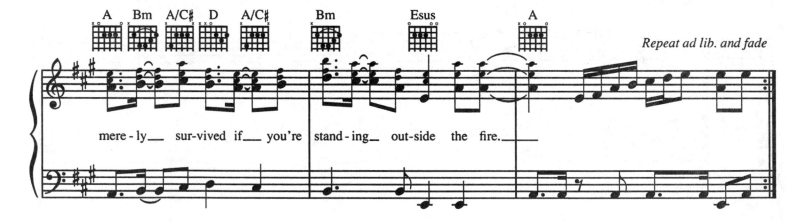

Verse 2:
We call them strong,
Those who can face this world alone,
Who seem to get by on their own,
Those who will never take the fall.
We call them weak,
Who are unable to resist
The slightest chance love might exist,
And for that forsake it all.
They're so hell bent on giving, walking a wire,
Convinced it's not living if you stand outside the fire.
(To Chorus:)

UNANSWERED PRAYERS

Words and Music by
LARRY B. BASTIAN, PAT ALGER
and GARTH BROOKS

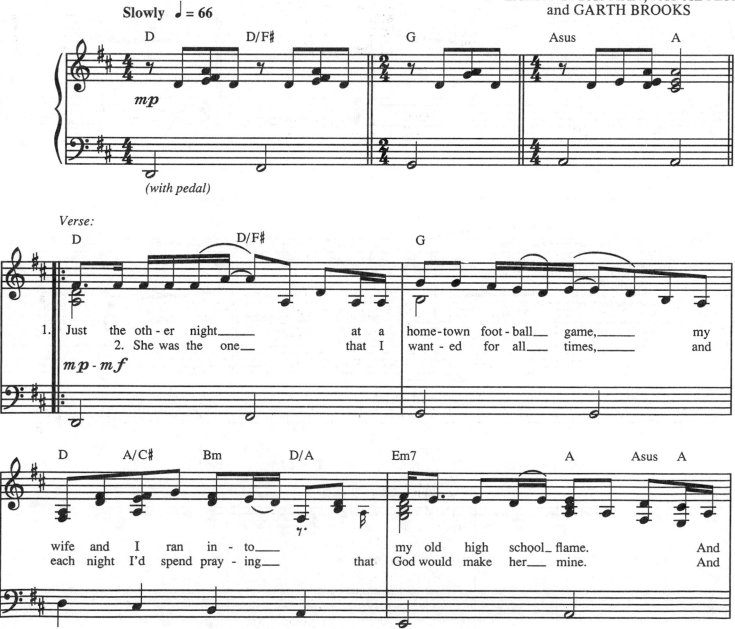

Slowly ♩ = 66

(with pedal)

Verse:

1. Just the oth-er night_____ at a home-town foot-ball_ game,_____ my
2. She was the one__ that I want-ed for all__ times,_____ and

wife and I ran in-to_____ my old high school_ flame. And
each night I'd spend pray-ing_____ that God would make her__ mine. And

Unanswered Prayers - 5 - 1

as I in - tro - duced_ them___ the past came back to me___ and I
if He'd on - ly grant_ me___ this wish I'd wished back then___ I'd

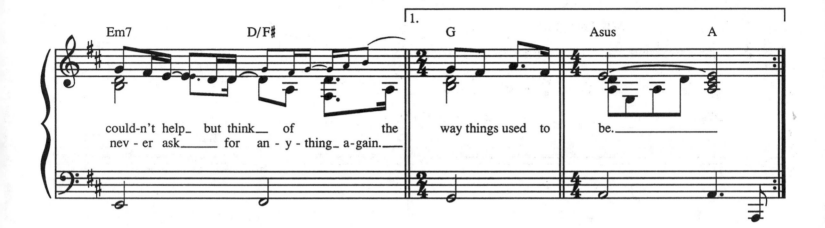

could-n't help_ but think_ of the
nev - er ask_ for an - y - thing_ a-gain.

way things used to be.___

Some-times I___ thank God___ for

un - an-swered prayers._ Re - mem-ber when you're talk - in' to the Man up - stairs_ that just be-cause_

He does-n't an - swer does-n't | mean He don't care,_____ | 'cause some of

To Coda ⊕

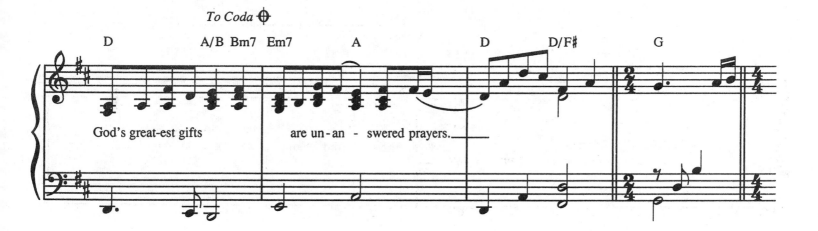

God's great-est gifts | are un - an - swered prayers._____

Verse:

3. She | was-n't quite the an - gel____ that I re -

mem-bered in my dreams,_____ | and I could | tell that time had changed_ me____ in

Unanswered Prayers - 5 - 3

her eyes too, it seemed.___ We tried to talk a-bout___ the old___ days,___ there was-n't

much we could___ re-call.___ I guess the Lord knows what he's do-ing af-ter

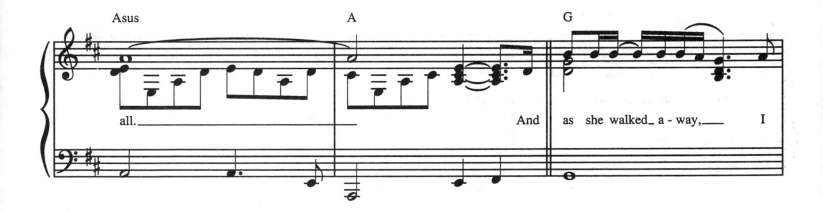

all._____ And as she walked___ a-way,___ I

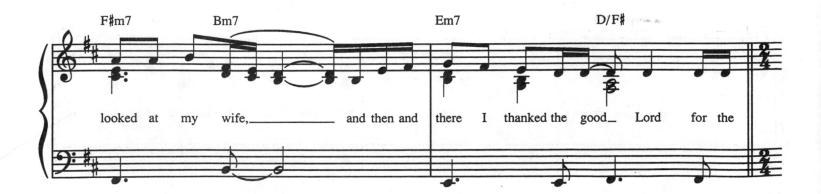

looked at my wife,_____ and then and there I thanked the good___ Lord for the

D.S. 𝄋 al Coda

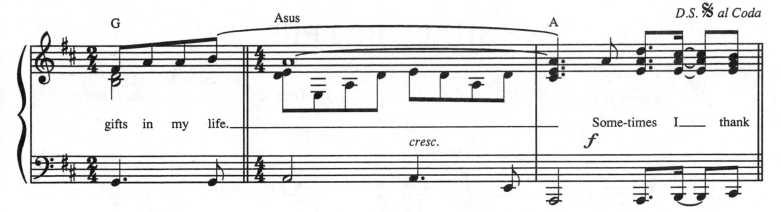

G   Asus   A

gifts in my life.   *cresc.*   *f*   Some-times I___ thank

⊕ *Coda*

Em7   A   D   A/B   Bm7

are un - an - swered,   some of God's great-est gifts   are all too

Em7   A7sus   A7   D   A/B   Bm7   Em7   A

of - ten un - an-swered,   some of God's great-est gifts   are un - an - swered prayers.___

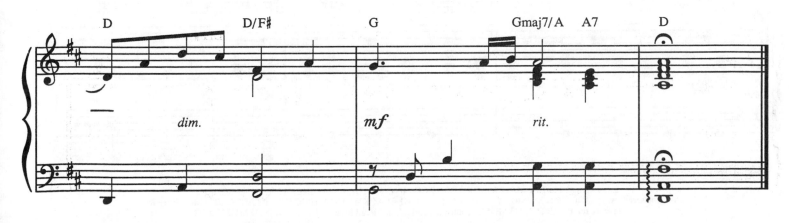

D   D/F♯   G   Gmaj7/A   A7   D

dim.   *mf*   *rit.*

WE SHALL BE FREE

Words and Music by
STEPHANIE DAVIS and GARTH BROOKS

We Shall Be Free - 5 - 1

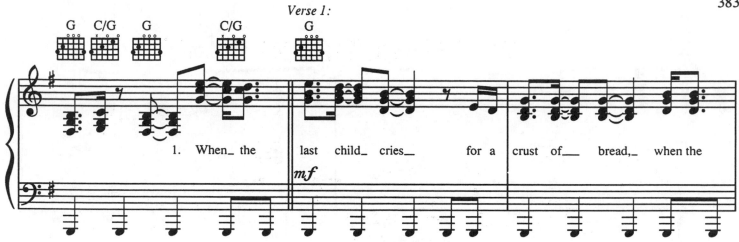

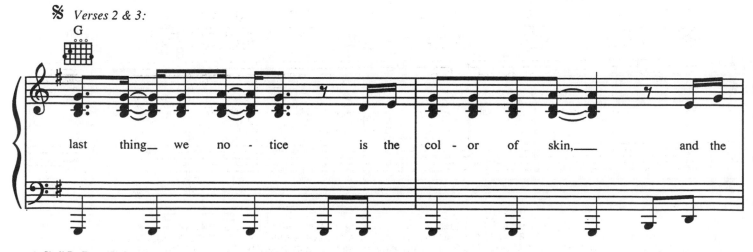

We Shall Be Free - 5 - 2

first thing___ we look___ for is the beau - ty with - in;_____ when the

skies___ and the o - ceans___ are clean a - gain,_____ then we shall___ be free.__

_ *cresc.* *f* 1. We shall___ be free,___

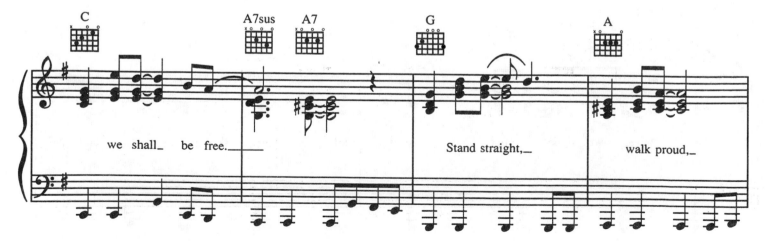

we shall___ be free.____ Stand straight,__ walk proud,__

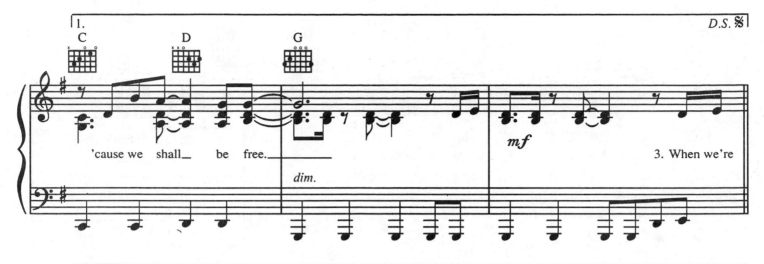

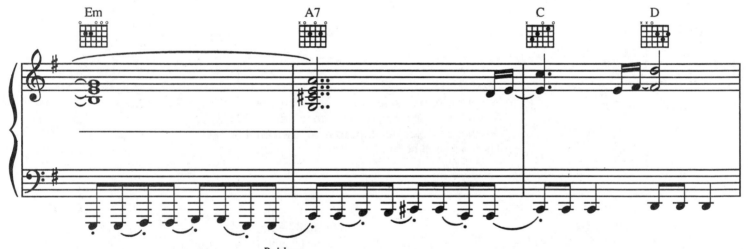

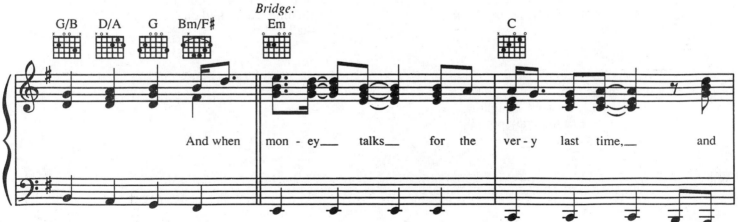

We Shall Be Free - 5 - 4

no - bod-y walks_ a step be - hind;_ when there's on - ly one race,_ and

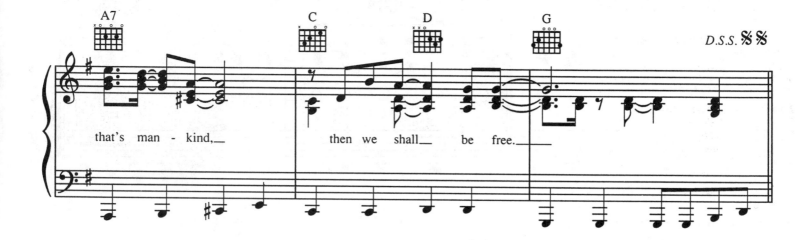

that's man - kind,_ then we shall_ be free._

D.S.S. 𝄋 𝄋

Verse 3:
When we're free to love anyone we choose,
When this world's big enough for all different views,
When we all can worship from our own kind of pew,
Then we shall be free.
(To Chorus:)

Chorus 2:
We shall be free,
We shall be free.
Have a little faith, hold out,
'Cause we shall be free.
(To Bridge:)

Chorus 3:
We shall be free,
We shall be free.
Stand straight, (walk proud,)
Have a little faith, (hold out;)
We shall be free.

Chorus 4:
We shall be free,
We shall be free.
(Stand straight,) stand straight,
(Have a little faith,) walk proud,
'Cause we shall be free.

Chorus 5:
Repeat Chorus 1 and fade

The Book of *Golden* Series

**THE BOOK OF GOLDEN
ALL-TIME FAVORITES**
(F2939SMX) Piano/Vocal/Chords

**THE BOOK OF GOLDEN
BIG BAND FAVORITES**
(F3172SMX) Piano/Vocal/Chords

**THE BOOK OF GOLDEN
BROADWAY**
(F2986SMX) Piano/Vocal/Chords

**THE NEW BOOK OF GOLDEN
CHRISTMAS**
(F2478SMB) Piano/Vocal/Chords
(F2478EOX) Easy Organ
(F2478COX) Chord Organ

**THE BOOK OF GOLDEN
COUNTRY MUSIC**
(F2926SMA) Piano/Vocal/Chords

**THE BOOK OF GOLDEN
HAWAIIAN SONGS**
(F3113SMX) Piano/Vocal/Chords

**THE BOOK OF GOLDEN
IRISH SONGS**
(F3212SMX) Piano/Vocal/Chords

**THE BOOK OF GOLDEN
ITALIAN SONGS**
(F2907SMX) Piano/Vocal/Chords

THE BOOK OF GOLDEN JAZZ
(F3012SMX) Piano/Vocal/Chords

**THE NEW BOOK OF GOLDEN
LATIN SONGS**
(F3049SMX) Piano/Vocal/Chords

**THE NEW BOOK OF GOLDEN
LOVE SONGS**
(F2415SOX) Organ

**THE BOOK OF GOLDEN
MOTOWN SONGS**
(F3144SMX) Piano/Vocal/Chords

**THE NEW BOOK OF GOLDEN
MOVIE THEMES, Volume 1**
(F2810SMX) Piano/Vocal/Chords

**THE NEW BOOK OF GOLDEN
MOVIE THEMES, Volume 2**
(F2811SMX) Piano/Vocal/Chords

**THE BOOK OF GOLDEN
POPULAR FAVORITES**
(F2233SMX) Piano/Vocal/Chords

**THE BOOK OF GOLDEN
POPULAR PIANO SOLOS**
(F3193P9X) Intermediate/
Advanced Piano

**THE BOOK OF GOLDEN
ROCK 'N' ROLL**
(F2830SMB) Piano/Vocal/Chords

**THE NEW BOOK OF GOLDEN
WEDDING SONGS**
(F2265SMA) Piano/Vocal/Chords